the GIGANTIC *book of* BASEBALL *Quotations*

ALSO AVAILABLE FROM SKYHORSE PUBLISHING

The Gigantic Book of Golf Quotations
The Gigantic Book of Fishing Stories
The Gigantic Book of Horse Wisdom
The Gigantic Book of Teachers' Wisdom
The Gigantic Book of Pirate Stories

the GIGANTIC *book of* BASEBALL *Quotations*

Edited and Introduced by WAYNE STEWART
Foreword by ROGER KAHN

Skyhorse Publishing

Skyhorse Publishing books may be purchased in bulk at special discounts for sales promotion, corporate gifts, fund-raising, or educational purposes. Special editions can also be created to specifications. For details, contact the Special Sales Department, Skyhorse Publishing, 307 West 36th Street, 11th Floor, New York, NY 10018 or info@skyhorsepublishing.com.

Visit our website at www.skyhorsepublishing.com.

10 9 8 7 6 5 4 3 2 1

Library of Congress Cataloging-in-Publication Data is available on file.

Cover design by David Ter-Avanesyan
Cover photos credit: Getty Images
Interior images by Getty Images

ISBN: 978-1-5107-6628-0
ebook ISBN: 978-1-5107-6965-6

Printed in the United States of America

CONTENTS

FOREWORD:
The Talkers' Game, by Roger Kahn

In his thoughtful and amiable work, *Diamond Classics: Essays on the 100 Best Baseball Books Ever Published*, Mike Shannon, the author-editor, describes baseball as "the writers' game." Within his 455 pages, Shannon underscores his point with comment on such worthies as Ring Lardner, James T. Farrell, Mark Harris, Bernard Malamud, Eliot Asinof, and George Plimpton, who could be quite good when he stopped focusing on himself. Shelves today variously bulge and sag under an increasing burden from ostensibly literary baseball anthologies.

Why does baseball write so well, probably better than any other sport?

Here are some factors:

Tradition. The major leagues trace back to the nineteenth century. One of my own favorite baseball books, Christy Mathewson's *Pitching in a Pinch*, appeared in 1912. In a reasonably literate society such as ours, books build on one another.

Leisurely pace. A good ballgame may last three hours, but no more than fifteen minutes is hard action. The rest of the time may be commercial space to the networks, but in the hands of a skillful author, it builds suspense.

Outsized characters. Mathewson, Ty Cobb, Babe Ruth, Leo Durocher, Joe DiMaggio, Jackie Robinson, Willie Mays. If an author can't write well about people like that, perhaps he had better peddle his keyboard and go into another field, say prawn diving.

Those, I suggest, are some reasons why baseball "writes." But my point here, and the point of this very considerable volume, is verbal. Baseball also "talks." No other sport comes close to matching baseball in jabber, prattle, impudence, abuse, wit, and sometimes even wisdom. Consider the folk who chatter in pages that follow:

- Hank Aaron, a man with a bat.
- Joe DiMaggio, as sure with one-liners as he was in center field.
- Bart Giamatti, a commissioner with a PhD.
- Shoeless Joe Jackson, eloquent in disgrace.
- Mickey Mantle, funny if not always printable.
- Walter O'Malley, who drove a spike through Brooklyn's heart.
- Branch Rickey, baseball's Winston Churchill.
- Red Smith, a genial sort and one of the most gifted sportswriters ever.
- Ted Williams, hit hard, lived hard, talked hard.

Listening to many of these people has been one of the pleasures of my several years. Since I believe that the words define the man, I've always taken pains to quote people accurately and this has created a number of perplexing situations. The most annoying is the Misquote Syndrome. That appears when someone has made a remark that gets into print and lets loose swarms of controversy. Caught in the furor, more than one baseball person has fallen back on what is for our purposes the big lie. "I never said that. Never even talked to the guy." A man who stood by quotes better than anyone else I encountered was Jackie Robinson. If a comment turned out to be ill-considered, Robinson might remark, "Maybe I shouldn't have said that, but I guess I did." Once Robinson said something, he stood by it. The worst on this issue of integrity? I don't want to be cruel, so no names here. Just initials. Pete Rose, the man whose word is worth its weight in fertilizer.

Sometimes an eager magazine editor calls and says he or she understands that bench jockeying is pretty funny stuff and would I write an article about it. Yes and no. For years most bench jockeying was either sexual or ethnic. During the 1934 World Series, Hank Greenberg told me, Dizzy Dean kept shouting at him, "Hey, Moe!" (Dean shouted from a distance. Greenberg was a large, powerful man.) Thus rattled, Greenberg batted .321 across the seven games. The sexual stuff has usually been primitive. "Hey, I was out with yer wife last night and she ain't so hot, either." Not uproarious, but what were you expecting, Groucho Marx? I've heard one or two very funny sexual wisecracks boiling out of dugouts, but each gets a triple-X rating, hardly fit for mainstream magazines. Since the ethnic stuff is offensive, and most of the sexual cracks are fit for adolescent locker rooms, if anywhere, I don't think bench jockeying offers a basis for a magazine story.

Some baseball quotes are so venerable, they can only be attributed to that notable source, A. Non. Who first yelled at a failing batter, "You swing like a rusty gate"? Who first shouted about a faltering pitcher, "Take him out"? (That cry, Christy Mathewson said, bothered him more than any other.) How many generations ago did a hitter foul a pitch into a foot and hop about, prompting bench jockeys to bark, "Arf, arf"? Or shout, "Hey, getcha hot dogs"? We don't know. We do know that this kind of noise is part of the game.

In this stout volume, Wayne Stewart has undertaken the formidable task of preparing a baseball equivalent to *Bartlett's Familiar Quotations*. He has obviously worked with great energy, taste, and passion for the sport. Perfect? There is no perfect book. I would have added to Stewart's source material two defunct New York newspapers, the *World* and the *Herald Tribune*. Each is a trove of baseball writing gold. To his list of magazines I would add the late *Saturday Evening* Post, which first published Ring Lardner's 1916 classic, *You Know Me, Al*.

But these are minor reservations about a wonderful piece of work. Besides, they may encourage Mr. Stewart to proceed with future editions. He has my best, and I hope his eyesight holds.

—Roger Kahn, April 2007
Stone Ridge, New York

INTRODUCTION

Admittedly, this book contains some quotations that are apocryphal and/or spurious; some are certainly contrived, manufactured. Take, for instance, one of the many lines Yogi Berra supposedly said: "I didn't really say everything I said." Pedro Guerrero's take was slightly different when he commented, "Sometimes they write what I say and not what I mean." The bottom line is as simple as the cliché "Don't believe everything you read."

Often, for example, once a quotation gets into circulation, it becomes accepted as the truth, whether the words were actually jotted down by, say, a ghostwriter; entirely fabricated by a reporter (said to be the case with "Say it ain't so, Joe."); or perhaps actually spoken by the subject then altered (consider the line "Nice guys finish last," discussed later).

Let's face it, baseball is notorious for building up legends, for putting words in players' mouths, and for embellishing both words and events. Who, for instance, could seriously believe that Willie Mays came up with such a line as "Baseball is a game, yes. It is also business. But what it most truly is is disguised combat. For all its gentility, its almost leisurely pace, baseball is violence under wraps." Gentility?! The word "gentility" from the "Say Hey Kid?" Forget about it.

This is the same Willie Mays who had Charles Einstein ghostwrite his biography, *My Life In and Out of Baseball*, yet, a short time after working with Einstein, forgot his name. According to Bert Sugar's *Rain Delays*, at the end of the 1965 season when Einstein gave his subject a follow-up call, after having taken notes with Mays throughout the season and after having identified himself over the phone, Mays said, "Charley who?" When Einstein prompted, "You know,

Charley Einstein, the fellow who is doing the book with you." Mays paused, then asked, "What book?"

It's not at all surprising either that some bursting-with-flavor quotes are attributed to different people, such as the great line about Mays's glove being where triples "go to die," which is listed in various sources as having been spoken by Vin Scully, Fresco Thompson, and Jim Murray. Some- times it's impossible to trace a great quotation toits true origin. In any event, baseball is richer for such classic comments, regardless of whoever first uttered them. Further, the vast majority of the quotes herein are right on the money regarding their legitimacy, their origin, and their purpose. Therefore, nitpicking aside, here are some of the funniest, wittiest, most poignant, most incisive, and most revelatory words ever written or spoken about the game of baseball.

—Wayne Stewart, December 2006
Lorain, Ohio

CHAPTER ONE

The Classic Quotes

For the purposes of this chapter, the definition of "classic" is a bit elastic, expanded somewhat, to be sure. Dictionaries consider something to be a classic if it serves as a standard of excellence and has survived the test of time, but another definition is "historically noteworthy, of special note." Likewise, as is the case with ESPN's term "instant classic," some of the gems in this chapter are young but seem certain to ultimately pass the "test" of time.

Other quotes in this chapter are irrefutable baseball classics such as the words a dying Lou Gehrig spoke: "Fans, for the past two weeks you have been reading about what a bad break I got. Yet today I consider myself to be the luckiest man on the face of the earth."

While a scant handful of men included here have names that are instantly recognizable, or usually associated with baseball, they are included, nevertheless, for their quotation contribution to the game.

Further, some lines are so old the precise origin of the quotation has been lost or muddled through the passage of time.

Sometimes, too, as mentioned in the foreword, a great line has been attributed to more than one person. No matter, these classic lines can cause one to chuckle, to ruminate, and possibly even to consider the game in a new light.

Baseball is too much of a sport to be called a business and too much of a business to be called a sport.

—Cubs owner Phil Wrigley

You can't steal first.

—Old baseball adage, supposedly first said by a manager who apparently wasn't fearful of Eddie Mayo's foot speed

It's a beautiful day for baseball.

—Attributed first to Cubs great Ernie Banks

A life is not important except in the impact it has on other lives.

—Dodgers standout Jackie Robinson

The trades you don't make are your best ones.

—Attributed to baseball executive Branch Rickey, also attributed to team owner Bill Veeck

I felt nothing. Nothing.

—Hall of Famer Ted Williams, when asked what he felt upon hitting his final homer in his last big-league trip to the plate

Luck is the residue of design.

—Baseball executive Branch Rickey

Records are made to be broken.

—Attributed to many

George Brett could roll out of bed on Christmas morning and hit a line drive.

—Royals general manager John Schuerholz; many variations of this have been used to describe many hitters over the years—e.g., "Rico Carty could wake up in the middle of the winter and get a base hit."

On a clear day they could see seventh place.

—Dodgers executive Fresco Thompson on the Phillies, c. 1920

Say it ain't so, Joe. Say it ain't so.

—Apocryphal line said to be uttered by a young boy to "Shoeless Joe" Jackson upon learning the 1919 World Series had been fixed and that Jackson took part in the scheme; Jackson was said to have replied, "Yes, kid, I'm afraid it is." Originally from the *Chicago Herald and Examiner*, September 30, 1920, and quoted in *Eight Men Out* by Eliot Asinof

A good umpire is the umpire you don't even notice.

—American League President Ban Johnson

Luck? If the roof fell in and Diz [Dean] was sitting in the middle of the room, everybody else would be buried and a gumdrop would drop in his mouth.

—Infielder Leo Durocher, from his book *Nice Guys Finish Last*

If you don't play to win, why keep score?

—Pirates pitcher Vernon Law

Mr. Rickey said, "Remember, it isn't the color of a man's skin that matters. It's what's inside the individual." And he said some of the people with the whitest skin would be the sorriest I'd meet and some of the darkest ones would be the best.

—Dodgers pitcher Preacher Roe, from *The Boys of Summer* by Roger Kahn

Which base?

—Reply of one Brooklyn fan to another who had informed him that "Da bums got three men on base."

It ain't over till it's over.

—Attributed to Yogi Berra, managing the Mets during the 1973 season

My epitaph is inescapable. It will read: "He sent a midget up to bat."

—Colorful team owner Bill Veeck

It ain't braggin' if you can do it.

—Brash pitcher Dizzy Dean

All I want out of life is that when I walk down the street, folks will say, "There goes the greatest hitter who ever lived."

—Boston superstar Ted Williams

Hit sign, win suit.

—Sign on Ebbets Field right-field wall advertising Abe Stark, Brooklyn tailor

THE PHILLIES USE LIFEBUOY [soap]

—Advertisement in Philadelphia's Baker Bowl that prompted fans to add, "but they still stink."

If he'd just tip his cap once, he could be elected mayor of Boston in five minutes.

—Hall of Famer Eddie Collins on Ted Williams

He ain't nothing till I say so.

—Umpire Bill Guthrie to a player insisting a baserunner was out

There is no defense against the walk.

—Traditional advice to pitchers

I didn't see it, but it sounded low.

—Attributed to outfielder Jim King, regarding a Moe Drabowsky fastball

Thou shalt not steal. I mean defensively. On offense, indeed thou shall steal and thou must.

—Branch Rickey, baseball executive

Baseball has to be a great game to survive the fools who run it.

—Hall of Famer Bill Terry

I'd rather be lucky than good.

—Pitcher Red Barrett, but also credited to standout pitcher Lefty Gomez

Attention, please: Will the people behind the rail in left field please remove their clothing.

—Brooklyn PA announcer requesting fans to remove items of clothing they had placed over a railing, distracting players

I couldn't have done it without my players.

—Manager Casey Stengel on his run of success with the Yankees

Fans, for the past two weeks you have been reading about what a bad break I got. Yet today I consider myself to be the luckiest man on the face of the earth.

—Yankees great Lou Gehrig at Yankee Stadium's "Lou Gehrig Day"

I never knew how someone dying could say he was the luckiest man in the world, but now I understand.

—Yankees great Mickey Mantle upon his retirement

Play me or keep me.

—Yankees utility man Phil Linz; also listed as "Bench me or keep me," and attributed to utility man Chico Salmon

I am pleased that God made my skin black, but I wish he had made it thicker.

—Outfielder Curt Flood

We Americans are a peculiar people. We are for the underdog no matter how much of a dog he is.

—Baseball commissioner Happy Chandler

It isn't really the stars that are expensive. It's the high cost of mediocrity.

—Team owner Bill Veeck

It's smarter to give the big man [Mickey Mantle] four balls for one base than one ball for four bases.

—Fellow Yankees outfielder Roger Maris

The key to winning is pitching, fundamentals, and three-run homers.

—Orioles manager Earl Weaver

When two old catchers meet on the street and shake hands, it takes a plumber 20 minutes to pry them apart.

—Former catcher Joe Garagiola

The two of them deserve each other. One's a born liar, the other's convicted.

—Manager Billy Martin on Reggie Jackson and George Steinbrenner

Rooting for the New York Yankees is like rooting for U.S. Steel.

—Sportswriter Red Smith; this line has also been attributed to comedian Joe E. Lewis

I imagine rooting for the Yankees is like owning a yacht.

—Sportswriter Jimmy Cannon

You can't tell how much spirit a team has until it starts losing.

—Tigers outfielder Rocky Colavito

[Stan] Musial's batting stance looks like a small boy looking around a corner to see if the cops are coming.

—Chicago White Sox pitcher Ted Lyons, 1941

Quick to think. Slow to anger.

—National League president Warren Giles to his umpires

Don't look back. Something might be gaining on you.

—Baseball legend Satchel Paige

It takes him an hour and a half to watch *60 Minutes*.

—Traveling secretary Donald Davidson, referring to Joe Niekro

Washington: First in war, first in peace, and last in the American League.

—Sportswriter Charles Dryden on the pathetic Washington Senators

I try not to break the rules but merely to test their elasticity.

—Team owner Bill Veeck

Nice guys finish last.

—Brooklyn manager Leo Durocher—although actually a misquote, this line has endured in baseball history.

Cut me and I'll bleed Dodger blue.

—Manager Tommy Lasorda

Wait till next year.

—Common Brooklyn Dodgers fans' saying

The first time I saw him, I thought he fell out of a Wheaties box.

—Announcer Joe Garagiola on Rick Reichardt

We finished last with you. We can finish last without you.

—First spoken by Pirates executive Branch Rickey to Ralph Kiner, who was holding out for more money

Is Brooklyn still in the league?

—Bill Terry, Giants manager, taunting a poor 1934 Dodger team—a team that would knock the Giants out of the pennant race

Cadillacs are down at the end of the bat.

—Pirates slugger Ralph Kiner, when asked why he didn't choke up for better contact

I took two of the most expensive aspirins in history.

—First baseman Wally Pipp, who, due to a headache, sat out, was replaced by Lou Gehrig, and then lost his job to Gehrig

It would depend on how well she was hitting.

—Pitcher Early Wynn responding, supposedly, to the question, "Would you throw at your own mother?" In another version of the tale, Wynn allegedly replied, "Only if she was digging in."

You gotta believe.

—Reliever Tug McGraw's battle cry

Because there is always some kid who may be seeing me for the first or last time. I owe him my best.

—Outfielder Joe DiMaggio on why he put out 100 percent every game

It's nothin' till I call it.

—Assertive umpire Bill Klem

I have discovered, in 20 years of moving around a ballpark, that the knowledge of the game is usually in inverse proportion to the price of the seats.

—Team owner Bill Veeck

The only time close counts is in horseshoes and dancing.

—Manager Fred Haney—this saying is sometimes listed as "close only counts in horseshoes and grenades" (attributed to Frank Robinson), also as ". . . in horseshoes and drive-in movies."

This must be the only job in America that everybody knows how to do better than the guy who's doing it.

—Umpire Nestor Chylak

CHAPTER TWO

Hitters and Hitting

Legendary hitting instructor Charlie Lau once said, "Nobody should hit .200. Anybody should [be able to] hit .250." In theory, perhaps, but in this chapter quotes flow not only from the stars of the game who soared well above the .200 and .250 strata, but also from a few men who would have infuriated Lau (initially and/or for their entire careers). There are even some observations from pitchers.

Hitting, after all, is a skill that has been studied for many a decade now, with some calling the study a science and others insisting hitting is more of an art. In any event, the topic has fascinated both players and fans alike since the dawn of the game.

For a man like Joe DiMaggio hitting involved, as he put it, no skill at all, "Just go up there and swing at the ball." Easy for him to say; this was a lifetime .325 hitter. For others, like pitcher Bob Buhl, hitting the ball crisply is a nearly impossible task.

Further, while pitching may well be the name of the game, fans, by and large, pack the ballparks to see hitters. Sure, many *claim* they love nothing better than taking in a classic pitchers' duel, but box office receipts belie that assertion and when baseball needs to boost attendance, they've been known to juice the ball or devise rules to shift the advantage to hitters.

There's a direct correlation between eras of hitting dominance and the rapid-fire clicking of big-league turnstiles. Look no further that the record-setting attendance figures of the late 1990s and into the 21st century.

Of course, we could look back in time, too. The demise of the Deadball Era, with none other than Babe Ruth dramatically plunging a knife into that period of baseball history with his long-ball exploits (an unheard of 29 homers in 1919, then an incredible 54 in 1920, followed by an ungodly 60 in 1927), gave birth to a golden era of power and the attendant bulging stadia.

When 1968 rolled around, "The Year of the Pitcher" was invasively thrust upon the baseball world. Bob Gibson's microscopic 1.12 ERA was an eye-popping performance and hitters were so befuddled only one American Leaguer hit .300. Baseball's response to the pendulum swing precipitously going the pitchers' way was the lowering of the mound. Since then virtually every significant rule change has favored hitters.

Hitters come in all shapes and sizes and their talents range from slugging with sheer unbridled power (think Ruth and Jimmie Foxx of long ago and Pete Alonso and Juan Soto of today) to guiding the ball through and over holes with diamond cutter precision à la Wee Willie Keeler, Paul Waner, Rod Carew, Wade Boggs, and Tony Gwynn.

The litany of hitters we loved to watch could fill a tome, a Pantheon—for that matter, a Hall of Fame. Like Stevie Wonder in his song "Sir Duke," which paid tribute to a slew of marvelous singers, we, too, can rattle off the names of our heroes: The Georgia Peach, the Sultan of Swat, Double-X, the Rajah, Hammerin' Hank, the Mick, and Charlie Hustle.

No doubt about it, fans not only cherish the game's hitting stars, they also love to hear what hitters have to say.

I keep a mental book on what pitchers throw me. When I'm hitting well, I can tell what a pitch will be when it's halfway to the plate.

—Hank Aaron, Braves superstar

When I hit a ball, I want someone else to go chase it.

—Hall of Famer Rogers Hornsby on why he didn't play golf

I'd rather try hitting a hummingbird than a knuckleball.

—Hitting great Pete Rose

Once [Stan] Musial timed your fastball, your infielders were in jeopardy.

—Pitching great Warren Spahn

Every great batter works on the theory that the pitcher is more afraid of him than he is of the pitcher.

—Tigers superstar Ty Cobb

There's a conspiracy among the clubs. Nobody's hiring thirty-seven-year-old players who can't hit.

—First baseman Mike Jorgensen

Mickey [Mantle] tried to hit every one like they didn't count under 400 feet.

—Yankees manager Casey Stengel

Most slumps are like the common cold. They last two weeks no matter what you do.

—Catcher Terry Kennedy

If [David] Ortiz were any more comfortable at the plate, he'd bring a chaise lounge, a pitcher of pina coladas and a couple of Cuban cigars with him to the batter's box.

—*New York Post* columnist Mike Vaccaro, from *Baseball Digest*, December 2006

I've never played drunk. Hung over, yes, but never drunk.

—Cubs outfielder Hack Wilson

Even his perspiration has muscles.

—First baseman Jimmie Foxx on Ted Kluszewski

One of these days [Frank] Howard will unleash a line drive at the opposing pitcher and the only identification left on the mound is going to be laundry mark.

—Team executive Fresco Thompson

A .220 hitter in the minors will be a .220 hitter all his life.

—Marty Marion as a Cardinals coach

In our day, he'd get knocked down. Whether it was [Babe] Ruth or anyone else swinging the bat good, we had a saying, "Let's see how he can hit lying on his back."

—Pitcher Elden Auker on how pitchers of the past would deal with Barry Bonds, from *www.webcircle.com*

They're all a bunch of crybabies, especially the small-change hitters.

—Umpire Doug Harvey

By trying to hit the ball back at the pitcher. In fact, I always tried to hit the ball back through the box, because that is the largest unprotected area.

—Hitting sensation Rogers Hornsby, when asked how he tried to come out of a hitting slump

I wasn't in a slump. I just wasn't getting any hits.

—Outfielder Dave Henderson

It's a round ball and a round bat and you got to hit it square.

—Reportedly first uttered by Seattle Pilots manager Joe Schultz; also attributed to Pete Rose and to Willie Stargell with the wording, "They give you a round bat and they throw you a round ball. And then they tell you to hit it square."

If ever a player deserved to hit .400, it's Ted [Williams]. He never sat down against tough pitchers. He never bunted. He didn't have the advantage of the sacrifice fly rule like those hitters before him.

—Boston teammate Joe Cronin

I heard a story that Joe Medwick . . . got himself beaned that time because he was tipped to a curve ball and it never curved. For myself, if I can get tipped to a pitch, most times I welcome it.

—Willie Mays, Hall of Famer, from *Willie Mays: My Life in and Out of Baseball* by Charles Einstein

It's not real comfortable hitting with two strikes. Guys don't like to get deep in the count because it takes away their aggressiveness if they get a strike or two on them.

—Infielder Walt Weiss, from *Baseball Digest*

I'm hitting so bad I could go into a slump and raise my average.

—Infielder Billy Grabarkewitz

Hitting is 50 percent above the shoulders.

—Hall of Famer Ted Williams

The way to fool [bad-ball hitter] Manny Sanguillen is to throw him right down the middle. He'll hit anything but a perfect pitch.

—Coach Billy DeMars

If he [Kirby Puckett] were playing in New York, there'd be a 5'8" statue of him in Times Square.

—Baseball executive Andy MacPhail

The only juicing Ryan [Howard] has ever done is apple or orange. Anyone who knows us can tell you that he is the smallest boy in the family.

—Chris Howard, older brother of 6'4", 252-pound slugger Ryan, from *Baseball Digest*, December 2006

Wait until [Jimmie] Foxx sees me hit.

—A young Ted Williams to writer Al Horwitz, who had just told Williams, "Wait till you see Jimmie Foxx hit," from *Red Smith on Baseball*, compiled by Phyllis W. Smith

You know you're going bad when your wife takes you aside and tries to change your batting stance. And you take her advice.

—Writer Thomas Boswell, from *How Life Imitates the World Series*

We weren't a very subtle team. We didn't pull a lot of squeeze plays. All we tried to do was hit the ball so hard it broke in half.

—Bobby Brown, Yankees third baseman, from *The Era* by Roger Kahn

A guy who strikes out as much as I do had better lead [the league] in something.

—Mike Schmidt, NL home run champ

You guys are trying to stop [Stan] Musial in 15 minutes when the National [League] ain't stopped him in 15 years.

—Catcher Yogi Berra to his pitchers at an All-Star Game

George Brett could get wood on an aspirin.

—Royals manager Jim Frey

If I'm hitting, I can hit anyone. If not, my twelve-year-old son can get me out.

—Pirates outfielder Willie Stargell

Once you get in that box, there's a certain sense of calm that players have and it's like a security blanket. You get in there and you don't think about anything else but trying to hit that ball.

—Outfielder Luis Gonzalez, from the *Arizona Republic*

When a guy hits a really long home run, there's a completely different sound. Then everybody stops. You look up and see the ball up there in the crowd with the hot dog vendors. The popcorn goes flying. The beer goes flying. It's a sweet thing.

—Hitting coach Tom McCraw

I see three baseballs, but I only swing at the middle one.

—Pirate great Paul Waner on hitting after a night out on the town

Your bat is your life. It's your weapon. You don't want to go into battle with anything that feels less than perfect.

—Outfielder Lou Brock

There has always been a saying in baseball that you can't make a hitter, but I think you can improve a hitter more than you can improve a fielder. More mistakes are made hitting than in any other part of the game.

—Hall of Famer Ted Williams

The bottom line is entertaining the fans, and watching some of our pitchers hit is pretty funny.

—Minnesota manager Tom Kelly

Anybody with ability can play in the big leagues. But to be able to trick people year in and year out the way I did, I think that's a much greater feat.

—Light-hitting catcher Bob Uecker

It's ridiculous that we are gathered here tonight to honor a man who made more than 7,000 outs.

—Pirates announcer Bob Prince, "roasting" Stan Musial upon his retirement

As far as I'm concerned, there is no greater pleasure in the world than walking up to the plate with men on base and knowing that you are feared.

—Hall of Fame catcher Ted Simmons

He was a hard out.

—Catcher Yogi Berra on Jackie Robinson

I was mowing my lawn during the baseball strike. I got the front yard done and about half the back, and then I kept waiting for Goose Gossage to come out and finish it for me.

—Pitcher Tommy John

He has muscles in his hair.

—Pitcher Lefty Gomez on slugger Jimmie Foxx

Mike [Piazza] turns mistakes into misery.

—Atlanta pitcher John Smoltz, from *The History of the New York Mets* by Michael E. Goodman

How hard is hitting? You ever walk into a pitch-black room full of furniture that you've never been in before and try to walk through it without bumping into anything? Well, it's harder than that.

—Cincinnati slugger Ted Kluszewski

[Baseball is] a hitter's game. They have pitchers because somebody has to go out there and throw the ball up to the plate.

—Relief pitcher Clay Carroll

Go up and hit what you see. And if you don't see anything, come on back.

—Washington manager Bucky Harris to his team on trying to hit Bob Feller

It was like a slow-pitch softball game. I can't believe some of those balls that went out.

—San Diego's Josh Barfield on the Dodgers' four straight homers to tie a game in the bottom of the ninth in 2006

If I just hit the fastball hard, it tells me I can handle his velocity that night. It also gives the pitcher the same thought.

—Long-ball hitter Mike Schmidt

[Eddie] Stanky couldn't hit, couldn't run, couldn't field, and couldn't throw, but he was still the best player on the club. All Mr. Stanky could do for you was win.

—Dodgers executive Branch Rickey

That's his style of hitting. If you can't imitate him, don't copy him.

—Catcher Yogi Berra on Frank Robinson

I got a big charge out of seeing Ted Williams hit. Once in a while they let me try to field some of them [his hits], which sort of dimmed my enthusiasm.

—Infielder Rocky Bridges

If I hadn't met those two at the start of my career, I would have lasted another five years.

—Yankees great Mickey Mantle on Whitey Ford and Billy Martin, his drinking buddies

When you're going like this [slumping], it looks like even the umpires have gloves.

—Reds star Pete Rose

It seems like every time he hits the ball, the thing comes off his bat like a stream of milk. He doesn't hit bloopers. Only screamers.

—Kansas City coach Frank Funk on George Brett

I've always been a patient hitter. I like to make the pitchers work. I don't like to give him any easy outs. If I can make him throw me four, five, or six pitches, and the other guys can do the same, that pitcher is going to be tired.

—All-Star second baseman Robbie Alomar, from *the Plain Dealer*, February 26, 2000

He hits the ball so hard the guy on deck can score.

—Boston's Mike Stanley on teammate Mo Vaughn

They're like sleeping in a soft bed. Easy to get into and hard to get out of.

—Star catcher Johnny Bench on slumps

My motto was always to keep swinging. Whether I was in a slump or feeling badly or having trouble off the field, the only thing to do was keep swinging.

—Hall of Fame outfielder Hank Aaron

I do know that when I'm not hitting, my wife could pitch and get me out.

—Outfielder Roger Maris

Not many people talk to you when you're hitting .195.

—Red Sox right fielder Dwight Evans, when asked if he was getting a lot of batting tips

It was an insurance run, so I hit it to the Prudential Building.

—Power hitter Reggie Jackson

I signed with the Milwaukee Braves for $3,000. That bothered my dad at the time, because he didn't have that kind of dough to pay out. But eventually he scraped it up.

—Catcher Bob Uecker

Everybody who roomed with [Mickey] Mantle said he took five years off his career.

—Pitcher Whitey Ford

He hit that so hard, he knocked the frogs off the Budweiser sign.

—Indians outfielder Brian Giles on a mammoth homer by Mark McGwire in Cleveland

George [Brett] throws a little fear into you. All you can do with him is hope he hits the ball at somebody and it isn't hard enough that it knocks your guy over.

—Manager Bobby Cox

Whatever they threw up there that season, George hit it. Pitches must have looked like beach balls to him.

—Kansas City star hitter Hal McRae on Brett's .390 season in 1980

The greatest thrill in the world is to end the game with a home run and watch everybody else walk off the field while you're running the bases on air.

—Al Rosen, Cleveland Indians great

[They] couldn't break a chandelier if they held batting practice in a hotel lobby.
—Pitcher Bill Lee on a weak-hitting Angels club

[As one ages,] you slow down and the infielders back up because they've got more time to throw you out at first. At the same time, you lose a little power, so the outfielders move in because you aren't hitting the ball so far. When they shake hands, you've had it.
—Outfielder Paul Waner

If I had my career to play over, one thing I'd do differently is swing more. Those 1,200 walks I got, nobody remembers them.
—Dodgers star Pee Wee Reese

I've heard of guys going 0-for-15, or 0-for-25, but I was 0-for-July.
—Infielder Bob Aspromonte

I'm up there with a bat and all the pitcher's got is the ball. I figure that makes it all in my favor. I let the fellow with the ball do the fretting.
—Hall of Famer Hank Aaron

A string of alibis.

—Manager Miller Huggins on what a slumping hitter needs

When I'm hitting, the ball comes up to the plate like a basketball. You can see the stitches and the writing on the ball. When you're not hitting, you don't see anything.

—Hall of Famer Rod Carew

[He's] the finest natural hitter in the history of the game.

—Ty Cobb on legendary outfielder "Shoeless Joe" Jackson

It would be useless for any player to attempt to explain successful batting.

—Hall of Fame outfielder Tris Speaker

He could hit buckshot with barbed wire.

—Royals manager Jim Frey on George Brett

I never saw anything like it. He doesn't just hit pitchers. He takes away their dignity.

—Dodgers Hall of Famer Don Sutton on Pirates slugger Willie Stargell

He's the only guy I know who can drive in three runs with nobody on base.

—Infielder Mark McLemore on Texas teammate Juan Gonzalez

Look for the seams and then hit in between them.

—Slugger Harmon Killebrew on how to hit a knuckleball

If someone threw him a rosin bag, he'd get a double.

—Manager Gene Mauch on Tom Paciorek

You're not always going to be perfect, but I always try to be.

—Hitting star Troy Glaus, *Baseball Digest*, October 2000

Players from both teams watch when Bo [Jackson] takes batting practice. There's always the feeling that you're going to see something you never saw before and we don't want to miss it.

—Bret Saberhagen, pitcher and Royals teammate of slugger Bo Jackson

With all the glamour attached to hitting the ball out of the park, it takes a lot of discipline to go up there and just try to get a base hit.

—Outfielder Garry Maddox

If Rod Carew has two strikes on him and fouls off five pitches and then takes the sixth down the middle, I'm calling it a ball.

—Umpire Ron Luciano

I've never seen anyone quite like this fellow. I saw Ted Williams do things with a baseball bat I'd never seen done before. I thought I'd never see better, but that was before I saw Carew.

—Manager Gene Mauch on Carew

With all the money I make now, I don't get my uniform any less dirty than when I was nine years old. The only difference is that my mother used to wash it.

—Hitting great Pete Rose

Yeah, you can pitch him low, but as soon as you throw the ball run and hide behind second base.

—Cleveland manager Lou Boudreau, when asked by a pitcher if he could pitch Ted Williams low, from *Baseball Is a Funny Game* by Joe Garagiola

Anybody with any sense knows that bats are like ballplayers—they hate cold weather.

—"Shoeless Joe" Jackson, hitting great

Don't forget to swing hard, in case you hit the ball.

—Cleveland infielder Woodie Held

Rick Dempsey is the kind of guy who would slide headfirst into an iron fence.

—Infielder Lee May

He has an uncanny ability to move the ball around as if the bat were some kind of magic wand.

—Pitcher Ken Holtzman on Rod Carew

I would be lost without baseball. I don't think I could stand being away from it as long as I was alive.

—Pirates batting champ Roberto Clemente

The only way I can't hit .300 is if there is something physically wrong with me.

—Pete Rose, as a young Reds infielder, c. 1963

The art of hitting is the art of getting your pitch to hit.

—Yankees infielder Bobby Brown

Due to the crowd [largest in Braves history] and the ceremony and my own burning desire to get it done, I felt like I had to break the record that night—and that I would.

—Hank Aaron on breaking Ruth's lifetime home run record in 1974, from *I Had a Hammer* by Hank Aaron with Lonnie Wheeler

What do you want, a higher average for me personally or value to the team? Every day, every at bat, I do what's good for the team, I move runners around and I knock runners in, but if you want batting average, I'll give it to you next year.

—Outfielder Tommy Heinrich on different ways hitting is judged, spoken during contract talks

The difference between this guy and the rest of us is that when we get hot, we go up to .300. When he gets hot, he goes up to .500.

—Angels star Doug DeCinces on Rod Carew

Buck hit a home run so far off Bob Feller that it cleared the fence, the bleachers, a row of houses, and hit a big old water tower out there. It rained in that town for five weeks.

—"Double Duty" Radcliffe of the Negro Leagues on hitting legend Buck Leonard

CHAPTER THREE

Pitchers and Pitching

Hitting aside, it is absolutely true that pitching is not only the name of the game, it is, according to experts such as the venerable Connie Mack, about "75 percent of baseball," and some place the percentage even higher. Good pitching has also been said to be so bedazzling that it can (and often does) simply overpower hitting. To use a baseball cliché, "Good pitching will always stop good hitting." Forget, for this chapter, another version of that quote that, after the words "good hitting," added the paradoxical phrase, "and vice versa."

It's hard to imagine now, in this age of 100-mph fastballs blazing downhill, but originally, by rule, a pitcher was in many ways a mere underhand lobber of offerings, not unlike slow-pitch softball pitchers. Further, there was a time when pitchers were required to, again, *by rule*, throw the ball either high or low as directed *by the batter*. Imagine, say, Mike Trout being permitted to shout out a decree to the mound, "I'd like another juicy pitch, say, belt high this time, thank you," with the pitcher having to comply!

After the turn of the century, the craft of pitching began to resemble what we've become accustomed to as the stars came out. Early luminaries included Walter Johnson, Christy Mathewson, Grover Cleveland Alexander, and even George Herman Ruth. Nearly a full century later, today's fans are entertained by the modern men of the mound—you've got Jacob deGrom, Trevor Bauer, Max Scherzer, et al.

Some pitchers' careers have been as ephemeral as the life of a mayfly (fittingly, also known as the "dayfly"). Cases in point: Minor league pitcher Stan Musial, who wound up pitching to just one batter at the big-league level. Then there were Smoky Joe Wood, who lasted only about seven full seasons and then, due to an arm injury, became an outfielder; obscure Hall of Famer Addie Joss, who experienced only five years with thirty or more starts and who died two days after his thirty-first birthday; and even Sandy Koufax, whose lifetime record stood at a mediocre 54–53 entering the 1962 season—he then rattled off a streak of five superlative seasons in which he led the league in ERA and tossed no-hitters seemingly effortlessly before bowing out prematurely at the age of 31.

Conversely, other pitchers have lasted for decades, allowing us to savor their mastery endlessly; Nolan Ryan and Clemens epitomize that kind of rare hurler.

Many of the quotes in this chapter pay homage to laser-like fastballs, relying heavily on hyperbole. Pirates announcer Bob Prince, for instance, spoke not only of pitchers who threw BBs and of fastballs that could penetrate a sturdy wall, but he took it one step beyond and regaled listeners with tales of men who could fire a *strawberry* through a brick wall. Other quotes deal with crafty pitchers, with the strategy of pitching, and so on.

Clearly, pitching is a colorful part of the game, a crucial key to victories. Likewise, quotations on pitching are often illuminating, amusing, and "winning" as well.

It got so I could nip frosting off a cake with my fastball.

—Hall of Fame pitcher Satchel Paige

A pitcher pitches low instead of high because how often have you seen a 420-foot ground ball?

—Pitcher Jim Bunning

Damn. Here I am trying to make a comeback and what do they tell me? My best pitch [his curve] is an optical illusion.

—Lefty Gomez, Yankees pitcher, on a *Life* magazine piece contending curveballs don't actually break

Pitchers, like poets, are born, not made.

—Cy Young, winner of a record 511 big-league games

The only thing he fears is sleep.

—Manager Jimmy Dykes on Don Larsen, said to tip a few drinks when not pitching

You haven't become a good pitcher until you can win when you don't have anything.

—Pitcher Sandy Koufax

Somebody will have to come out and take the uniform off me and the guy who comes after it had better bring help.

—Feisty pitcher Early Wynn, regarding his retirement

I don't know. My eyes were closed.

—Atlanta pitcher Tommy Boggs, when asked what pitch he had slugged for a homer

I threw the ball so hard I tore a couple of boards off the grandstand. One of the fellows said that the stand looked like a cyclone struck it. That's how I got the name, and it was shortened to Cy.

—Pitching great Cy Young

It's like I said at Satchel's funeral in 1982: people say it's a shame he never pitched against the best. But who's to say he didn't?

—Negro Leagues star Buck O'Neil on Satchel Paige

Home plate is seventeen inches wide, but I ignore the middle twelve. I pitch to the two-and-a-half inches on each side.

—Pitching great Warren Spahn

We developed a very scientific system for bringing in relief pitchers. We used the first one who answered the telephone.

—Pitching coach Chuck Estrada

You never have too much pitching.

—General manager Frank Cashen

You gotta keep the ball off the fat part of the bat.

—Pitcher Satchel Paige

[Don] Gullett's the only guy who can throw a baseball through a car wash and not get the ball wet.

—Reds star Pete Rose on his teammate

Can I throw harder than Joe Wood? Listen, mister, no man alive can throw any harder than Smoky Joe Wood.

—Hall of Fame pitcher Walter Johnson

I think I've got a great shot at 20 wins—I mean, I'm 19–23 now, so I've only got one [win] to go.

—Pitcher Dave Heaverlo of winning 20 games, *lifetime* (he wound up 26–26)

Blind people come to the park just to listen to him pitch.

—Slugger Reggie Jackson on Tom Seaver

I felt like shouting out that I had made a ball curve. I wanted to tell everybody; it was too good to keep to myself.

—Pitcher Candy Cummings, credited as the first player to discover and throw a curve

I pitch like my hair's on fire.

—Reliever Mitch Williams, also attributed to Cubs teammate Mark Grace, who said, "Mitch pitches like his hair's on fire"

Look at him. He [Willie Mays] knows he's going to hit me and I know he's going to hit me, so I'm going to walk him.

—Pitcher Harvey Haddix (to his catcher)

I've seen guys pitch bad and I've seen guys pitch in bad luck, but you've done an outstanding job of putting it all together.

—Texas pitcher Sparky Lyle to teammate Jim Kern

Really, what does ERA mean anymore? Honestly. We're in smaller parks, the guys are huge, and they're hitting Titleists.

—Pitcher Tim Belcher, c. 2000

Teams can't prepare for me in batting practice—they can't find anyone who throws as slow as I do.

—Pitcher Dave LaPoint

A man should always hold something in reserve, a surprise to spring when things get tight.

—Pitcher Christy Mathewson

I'm working on a new pitch—it's called a strike.

—Pitcher Jim Kern

A faint heart is one of the big causes of sore arms.

—Frank Foreman, nineteenth-century Orioles pitcher

I throw the ball right down the middle. The high-ball hitters swing over it and the low ball hitters swing under it.

—Pitcher Saul Rogovin, whose career was right down the middle, too, at 48–48

Trying to hit Phil Niekro is like trying to eat Jell-O with chopsticks. Once in a while you might get a piece, but most of the time you go hungry.

—Outfielder Bobby Murcer

You can take a nap in between [Hideo Nomo's] pitches.

—Outfielder Gary Sheffield

When Neil Armstrong set foot on the moon, he found a baseball that Jimmie Foxx hit off me in 1937.

—Pitcher Lefty Gomez

I can't throw one, so I bought one.

—Pitcher Curt Schilling, after buying a dog and naming it Slider

Pitching, to me, is throwing strikes and throwing strikes down low. To be able to throw a fastball on the inside part of the plate and then on the outside part of the plate, within a range of two or three inches—that's big league control.

—Mets ace Tom Seaver, from *The History of the New York Mets* by Michael E. Goodman

Trying to lift Carl Hubbell's screwball was like a guy trying to hit fungoes out of a well.

—Manager Frankie Frisch, from *Baseball Digest*

I throw the ball harder than Nolan Ryan. It just doesn't get there as fast.

—Pitcher Steve Busby

There is nothing so dead as a dead arm.

—Catcher Benny Bengough

That's sinful. You're sitting there and the guy is clocking 103 miles per hour, 102. He never goes less than 100.

—Former Tigers manager Sparky Anderson on Detroit fireballer Joel Zumaya

He threw the ball as far from the bat and as close to the plate as possible.

—Manager Casey Stengel on Satchel Paige

That last one sounded a little low.

—Pitcher Lefty Gomez of a called strike three from Bob Feller

I don't cheat out there—at least I don't get caught.

—Tigers pitcher Milt Wilcox

Pitching is really just an internal struggle between the pitcher and his stuff. If my curveball is breaking and I'm throwing it where I want, then the batter is irrelevant.

—Cy Young Award winner Steve Stone

I've won more games than you've ever seen.

—Cy Young, winner of 511 games

I don't, but neither does the batter.

—Pirates relief specialist Roy Face when asked if he knew which way his famed forkball would break

Without the deception of the curve, baseball would have become just another sport for young men of premium size and strength.

—Writer Martin Quigley

Whatever they [catchers] put down, I threw, but you learn to trust yourself and your ability. You have to pitch the way you did in the minors, the way that got you here. It comes with confidence. [Later] you'll shake the catcher off. You know what you can do.

—Cleveland pitcher Charles Nagy, from *Indians on the Game* by Wayne Stewart

Submarine pitchers can give you an inning or two seventy times a year.

—Reliever Steve Reed, from *Baseball Digest*, November 2000

When Mickey Mantle bunted with the wind blowing out in Crosley Field.

—Pitcher Robin Roberts of his biggest All-Star Game moment

A guy who throws what he intends to throw—that's the definition of a good pitcher.

—Hall of Fame pitcher Sandy Koufax

You're standing on two tons of dirt. Why don't you rub some of it on the ball?

—Mets manager Casey Stengel to his pitcher, who said he was having trouble gripping the ball

He's baseball's exorcist—he scares the devil out of you.

—Detroit outfielder Dick Sharon on Nolan Ryan

Throw high risers at the chin; throw peas at the knees; throw it here when they're lookin' there; throw it there when they're lookin' here.

—Pitching legend Satchel Paige

You could catch him with a pair of pliers.

—Catcher Ed Bailey on Stu Miller's lack of speed

A pitcher needs two pitches—one they're looking for and one to cross them up.

—Warren Spahn, winningest lefty ever

Why me? I don't smoke. I don't drink. I don't run around. Baseball is my whole life. Why me?

—Dodgers pitcher Ralph Branca's lament after giving up the pennant-winning home run to Bobby Thomson in 1951

He's a guy who knows how to pitch. He works the corners; he works the change of speed. He gets guys to chase balls that other guys can't get them to chase. And he pitches to the angles of the ballpark. He's become a thinker pitcher.

—Oakland's Frank Thomas in 2006 on Tigers hurler Kenny Rogers, from *USA Today Sports Weekly*

I don't know. I've never pitched in a phone booth before.

—Pitcher Gene Conley, when asked how he'd like pitching in Fenway Park

I have never considered myself a great talent. I think I have gotten more publicity for doing less than any other player who ever lived.

—Pitcher Bo Belinsky

When I saw the left-field fence, I thought we were going to play softball.

—Pitcher Joaquin Andujar on Fenway Park

If running [to prepare pitchers] is so important, Jesse Owens would be a 20-game winner.

—Pitching coach Art Fowler

[Justin] Verlander is tough. He reminds me of Jack Morris when he first came up.

—Tigers outfielder Willie Horton

There is nothing quite like the feeling of expectation on the morning of the day or night that you are scheduled to pitch.

—Hall of Famer Tom Seaver

In my era, you've got Roger Clemens, Randy Johnson, Greg Maddux—but as far as I'm concerned, Pedro's the best.

—Pitcher Bret Saberhagen on Pedro Martinez, from *The History of the Boston Red Sox* by Aaron Frisch

They've got a lot of names for pitches now, but there are only so many ways you can throw a baseball.

—Pete Reiser, as a Cubs coach

My mother told me never to put my dirty fingers in my mouth.

—Pitcher Don Drysdale, contending he didn't load up on the ball

I've had pretty good success with Stan [Musial]—by throwing him my best pitch and backing up third.

—Dodgers pitcher Carl Erskine

He could thread a needle with that ball.

—Les Bell, infielder, on Grover Cleveland Alexander

They ain't no such animal. Anybody's best pitch is the one the batters ain't hitting that day. And it doesn't take long to find out.

—Pitching great Christy Mathewson

There is a pitch in baseball much different from the fastball that "separates the men from the boys." If this pitch does not curve, it would be well to notify a lot of baseball players who were forced to quit the game they love because of this certain pitch.

—Manager Eddie Sawyer on the concept that the curve is an optical illusion, from "The Hell It Don't Curve" by Joseph F. Drury Jr. in *The American Mercury Magazine*, reprinted in *The Baseball Reader* by Charles Einstein

He once hit me in the on-deck circle.

—Second baseman Billy Herman on intimidating pitcher Freddie Fitzsimmons

Yeah, but I defy anybody to throw him a good ball.

—Tigers pitcher Hal Newhouser after being told Yogi Berra is a notorious bad-ball hitter

You can't have a miracle every day—except you can when you get great pitching.

—Manager Casey Stengel

Mike [Cuellar] always thinks two pitches ahead. When they make an out on one of his "set-up" pitches, he looks like they've spoiled his fun.

—Elrod Hendricks, Orioles catcher

The Chief's glare scared me and we were on the same team.

—Pitcher Whitey Ford of Yankees teammate Allie Reynolds

That's like asking if I'd rather be hung or go to the electric chair.

—Baltimore's Merv Rettenmund, when asked if he'd rather hit against Tom Seaver or Jim Palmer

Everybody thinks that all the places he [Gaylord Perry] touches are decoys. I don't think any are decoys. I think he's got that stuff [illegal substances] everywhere.

—Manager George Bamberger

When Sandy Koufax retired.

—Pirates great Willie Stargell, when asked what his biggest thrill in baseball was

Today's athletes run faster and make a lot more plays in the field, but the name of the game is pitching and it ain't going to change. Pitching was 80 percent of baseball when John McGraw managed and it's still 80 percent of baseball.

—Manager Paul Richards

There's smoke coming out of his nose and his cap is down over his eyes and he's so big and hulking. You need a cape to face [Goose] Gossage, not a baseball bat.

—Infielder and outfielder Tom Paciorek

Umpires are most vigorous when defending their miscalls.

—Pitcher Jim Brosnan

The space between the white lines—that's my office. That's where I conduct my business.

—Intimidating pitcher Early Wynn

One day I was pitching against Washington and the catcher called for a fastball. When it got to the plate, it was so slow that two pigeons were roosting on it. I decided to quit.

—Pitcher Dizzy Trout

I hated to bat against [Don] Drysdale. After he hit you, he'd come around, look at the bruise on your arm and say, "Do you want me to sign it?"

—Yankees great Mickey Mantle

After a while, I asked if I could pitch from closer in.

—Knuckleball pitcher Charlie Hough after giving up five consecutive walks

I have no idea. Roll it up there and hope it doesn't bounce.

—Manager Jim Leyland on how to pitch to Mark McGwire

Pitch him low.

—Tigers catcher Bob Swift, instructing his pitcher how to throw to 3'7" Eddie Gaedel, who had one major league at-bat

He has the power to throw the ball through a wall, but you couldn't be quite sure which building.

—Manager Casey Stengel on the erratic but blazing fastballer Rex Barney, from *Baseball's Funniest People* by Michael J. Pellowski

It's pretty bad when your family asks for passes to the game and wants to sit in the left-field bleachers.

—Twins pitcher Bert Blyleven, single-season record holder for the most homers surrendered

What's the use of doing in three pitches what you can do in one.

—Pitching great Grover Cleveland Alexander, minimizing the importance of strikeouts

For the first sixty feet it was a hell of a pitch.

—Hall of Fame pitcher Warren Spahn on a home run he served up to Willie Mays

How can I intimidate batters if I look like a golf pro?

—Reliever Al Hrabosky after his team told him to shave his facial hair

I became a good pitcher when I stopped trying to make them miss the ball and started trying to make them hit it.

—Dodgers great Sandy Koufax

If Diz [Dizzy Dean] ever gets smart, he's through.

—Manager Paul Richards

I exploit the greed of all hitters.

—Braves star pitcher Lew Burdette

Whitey [Ford] was a master. It was like watching a pitching textbook in the flesh.

—Yankees pitcher Ralph Terry

Never win 20 games, because then they expect you to do it every year.

—Colorful pitcher Billy Loes, also listed at times as "I have no intention or desire to win 20 games, because they keep expecting it of you.

Connie Mack, who has seen more ballgames than any other American, living or dead, always considered Young's perfect game against Rube Waddell in 1904 the greatest exhibition of pitching ever performed.

—Sportswriter Tom Meany on Cy Young

My earned run average is so high, it looks like an AM radio station.

—Pitcher Jim Gott

He got hit so hard I had to get all the married men off the field.

—Manager Whitey Herzog on pitcher Ken Dayley

Mother was a hell of a hitter.

—Pitcher Early Wynn on being labeled a pitcher who "wouldn't give his mother a good pitch to hit."

If you can cheat, I wouldn't wait one pitch longer.

—Orioles pitching coach George Bamberger to pitcher Ross Grimsley, in a jam (also attributed to Earl Weaver telling Grimsley, "If you know how to cheat, start now.")

That's better, anyway you look at it, than someone calling you a shoeshine boy.

—Pitcher Sal Maglie on his nickname, "the Barber"

Hitting is timing. Pitching is upsetting timing.

—Warren Spahn, Hall of Fame hurler

I want to thank my teammates who scored so many runs and Joe DiMaggio, who ran down my mistakes.

—Yankees pitcher Lefty Gomez

I don't put any foreign substance on the baseball. Everything I use on it is from the good ol' USA.

—Cubs pitcher George Frazier on his spitball

It gives them [hitters] a lot more to think about. . . . He'd throw it twice and you'd be looking for it on 116 pitches.

—Orioles manager Earl Weaver on Gaylord Perry and his spitball

I don't want to get to know the other guys too well. I might like them and then I might not want to throw at them.

—Intimidating pitching star Sal "the Barber" Maglie on why he didn't fraternize with opposing players, from *Baseball Is a Funny Game* by Joe Garagiola

He's left-handed and he's breathing.

—Minnesota manager Tom Kelly on why they drafted a less-than-stellar pitcher

Why pitch nine innings when you can get just as famous pitching two?

—Relief pitcher Sparky Lyle

Whenever he came into a game people would stop eating their popcorn.

—Manager Casey Stengel on the fast but erratic pitcher Ryne Duren

If it was, more pitchers would be soaking their heads instead of their arms.

—Pitcher Jim Lonborg when asked if pitching was more mental than physical

I knew it would ruin my arm, but one year of 25–7 is worth five years of 15–15.

—Orioles pitcher Steve Stone

He touches the bill of his hat, then the back of his hat, then he'll dig around in his glove; guys are so busy trying to figure out where he's hiding the stuff [illegal substances] that they forget to try and hit him.

—Cleveland outfielder Oscar Gamble on teammate Gaylord Perry, from *The History of the Cleveland Indians* by Richard Rambeck

My best pitch is one I do not throw.

—Spitball artist Lew Burdette, denying he loaded up his pitches

Sometimes he [Roger Clemens] forgets that he's a human being. I have to remind him that even a pitching machine throws a bad one every once in a while.

—Pitching coach Bill Fischer

If you let him get a head of steam by the seventh inning, you can't hit him. You can't even see him.

—Pitching coach Larry Sherry on Nolan Ryan

Everybody who pitches, pitches with some pain. . . . I would throw a pitch and it would hurt, but then the pain would go away—until the next pitch.

—Cardinals great Bob Gibson

Don Drysdale would consider an intentional walk a waste of three pitches. If he wants to put you on base, he can hit you with one.

—Cardinals infielder Mike Shannon

We've finally found the perfect short man.

—Cubs pitcher Dave Smith, joking about the mop-up pitching 5'8" outfielder Doug Dascenzo had performed

My three pitches: my change, my change off my change, and my change off my change off my change.

—Dodgers pitcher Preacher Roe on his slow stuff

It's the difference between a carpenter and a cabinetmaker.

—Manager Birdie Tebbetts on the difference between raw, rookie pitchers and veteran hurlers

I'll tell you, you can't live off a fastball alone.

—Royals pitcher Dennis Leonard

His stuff was nasty. But what you really noticed was that he pitched mean . . . this man doesn't just want to get batters out, he wants to laugh at them.

—Royals slugger John Mayberry on teammate Steve Busby

I always felt the pitcher had the advantage, like serving in tennis.

—Yankees pitcher Allie Reynolds

A pitcher has to look at the hitter as his mortal enemy.

—Early Wynn, pitcher famous for his fiery temper

He can make the ball look so small that you're not even sure there's a practical purpose for being up there [at the plate].

—Orioles outfielder John Lowenstein on Goose Gossage

I'd always have it [illegal substances] in at least two places, in case the umpires would ask me to wipe one off. I never wanted to be caught out there without anything. It wouldn't be professional.

—Cy Young Award–winning Gaylord Perry on his spitball,
from *Me and the Spitter* by Perry with Bob Sudyk

There you is and there you is going to stay.

—Pitcher Satchel Paige after issuing a walk to a leadoff hitter;
he fanned the next three men

A pitcher who walks Babe Ruth throws a party. A pitcher who walks Freddie Patek wants to go home and kick the dog.

—Royals manager Whitey Herzog

I hit a foul ball off Pedro and I was happy. I could hear the crowd cheer.

—Veteran catcher Sandy Alomar Jr. on pitcher Pedro Martinez

I never say "seven-fifteen" anymore. I now say "quarter after seven."

—Pitcher Al Downing, the man who surrendered record-breaking home run number 715 to Hank Aaron

I was a bonus baby. I got two autographed baseballs and a scorecard from the 1935 All-Star Game.

—Cleveland pitcher Bob Feller

Relief pitching is the penthouse or the warehouse. Sometimes you throw three average pitches and get three outs. Then you throw 10 good ones, but two or three are bad ones and you end up like I did tonight.

—Veteran pitcher Jim Kaat in 1980

I'm not saying nobody else has had a better curve [ever]—Camilo Pascual had a really good one and Mike Witt has a great one now—but I have never caught anybody with a better curveball than Bert's.

—Don McMahon, pitching coach, on Bert Blyleven
from *Baseball Digest*, March 1985

The owners think if I wasn't in baseball I'd be out digging ditches or something. That really fries me. How can they be in baseball and not see what it's all about? Pitching is a beautiful thing. It's an art.

—Hall of Famer Tom Seaver

What I do is mentally picture myself pitching to a batter and striking him out. Then, I work myself into a hate mood and make it a personal battle between me and the batter.

—Reliever Al "the Mad Hungarian" Hrabosky

Comparing me with Sandy Koufax is like comparing Earl Scheib with Michelangelo.

—Pitcher Don Sutton

You could catch him in a rocking chair. He had two important requirements: good control and a good disposition.

—Catcher Bob O'Farrell on Carl Hubbell

Don's idea of a waste pitch is a strike.

—Pitcher Jim Brosnan on Don Drysdale

I'm always amazed when a pitcher becomes angry at a hitter for hitting a home run off him. When I strike out, I don't get angry at the pitcher, I get angry at myself.

—Pirates star Willie Stargell

The league will be a little drier now.

—Gaylord Perry upon his retirement

He [Walter Johnson] could throw the ball by you so fast you never knew whether you'd swung under it or over it.

—Pitcher Smoky Joe Wood

A pitcher does this once in a lifetime—once in baseball history—and we can't win the game for him.

—Pirates outfielder Bill Virdon on Harvey Haddix's losing a perfect game in extra innings

I can see how he won 25 games. What I don't understand is how he lost five.

—All-Star catcher Yogi Berra on Dodger great Sandy Koufax's stellar 1963 season

An elevated game of catch.

—Pitching coach Ray Miller's definition of pitching, from *Baseball Digest*, September 1990

The pitcher is the happiest with his arm idle. He prefers to dawdle in the present, knowing that as soon as he gets on the mound and starts his windup he delivers himself to the uncertainty of the future.

—Author George Plimpton, from *Out of My League*

Tommy's curveball had a better hangtime than Ray Guy's punts.

—Manager Rocky Bridges on minor league pitcher Tommy Lasorda

The only thing Earl knows about pitching is that he couldn't hit it.

—Orioles pitcher Dave McNally on Baltimore manager Earl Weaver, also attributed to pitcher Jim Palmer

His pitches remind me of the garbage I take out at night.

—Hitting great Rod Carew on Mike Boddicker

What do you mean, pressure? In New York, I pitched once when we were trying to keep from losing a hundred games. That's pressure.

—Mets hurler Nino Espinosa

It was like talking to Thomas Edison about light bulbs.

—Knuckleball pitcher Tom Candiotti on having the opportunity to ask knuckleball artist Phil Niekro for advice

He had the stubbornness of a mule and the grace of a thoroughbred.

—Tiger manager Sparky Anderson on ace pitcher Jack Morris

I feel like Job. I can't get mad at anybody except the Lord and if I do that I'm afraid things will get worse.

—Hall of Famer Sandy Koufax after getting injured

Randy's pitches are too good to take and not good enough to hit.

—Coach Bob Skinner of Padres pitcher Randy Jones

It's no fun throwing fastballs to guys who can't hit them. The real challenge is getting them out on stuff they can hit.

—Cleveland pitcher Sam McDowell

When you talk velocity, Nolan threw the hardest. In 1973, Nolan threw a pitch a little up and over my left shoulder. I reached up for it and Nolan's pitch tore a hole in the webbing of my glove and hit the backstop at Fenway Park.

—Jeff Torborg on catching all-time strikeout king Nolan Ryan

They called it a Cuban fastball back then [in Gaylord Perry's early pitching days] until they stopped getting guys from Cuba who threw it. Then they just called it a fork ball.

—Ace pitcher Gaylord Perry, contending his spitball was really a fork ball, from *Pitching Secrets of the Pros* by Wayne Stewart

Show me a guy who can't pitch inside and I'll show you a loser.

—Hall of Fame pitcher Sandy Koufax

I had most of my trouble with left-handed hitters. Charlie Gehringer could hit me in a tunnel at midnight with the lights out.

—Pitching great Lefty Gomez

It doesn't matter how many you walk so long as they don't score.

—Nolan Ryan on his occasional wildness

If a pitcher feels he has been intimidated by a hitter, he has a right to throw at him.

—Pitcher Lynn McGlothen

All that jumping around, tipping their hats, shaking hands with the fans—I might knock down more of them [hitters] today than when I pitched. I wouldn't waste a pitch hitting them either. I'd hit 'em in the dugout.

—Pitching great Early Wynn on "showboating" players

The way I look at it, a home run is just a fly ball that goes a little farther.

—Mets star pitcher Ron Darling

My boy, I can't recall anyone loading the bases against me.

—Pitching great Cy Young when asked what his out pitch was with bases loaded

Are you talking about Picasso? That's what I call him. When a guy can throw the ball where he wants to, anywhere, on any pitch, at any time in the count, that's painting. And no one paints like Maddux.

—Arizona outfielder Luis Gonzalez on Greg Maddux

I can't spread my fingers that far apart so I didn't mess with it—I didn't need it.

—Pitching great Bob Gibson on the split-finger fastball

Fact is, I've got so much speed today, I'll burn up the catcher's glove if I don't let up a bit.

—Pitching great Rube Waddell

If it's easy to teach, it's hard to hit.

—Manager Mike Hargrove on the splitter, from *Pitching Secrets of the Pros* by Wayne Stewart

The relief pitcher is the one man on a team that can make a manager look like a genius.

—Reds skipper Birdie Tebbetts

You don't want a knuckleballer pitching for you. Of course, you don't want one pitching against you either.

—Manager Paul Richards

The pitcher has to find out if the batter is timid. And if the hitter is timid, he has to remind the hitter he's timid.

—Pitcher Don Drysdale on throwing inside

I have four basic pitches: fastball, curve, slider, and change-up, plus eight illegal ones.

—Pitcher Tommy John

I love watching this guy, especially on TV, because he carves up hitters like a surgeon. As a pitcher, the most important thing is location. The second most important thing is the movement of the pitch. The last thing is velocity.

—Former pitcher and manager Larry Dierker on Greg Maddux

My fastball, my slider, my ERA, and my blood pressure.

—Pitcher Rich Gale, when asked, "What's up?"

I'm like a machine out there, just throwing pitch after pitch as quickly as I can. My mind's in neutral. I've got only one pitch [his splitter], so it doesn't matter who the hitter is.

—Reliever Bruce Sutter

I was 1–9. With any luck I'd have been 2–7.

—Pitcher Jim Bouton

I don't like to give in to the batter, that's just my personality. I challenge them. If they hit it, make it be a solo shot. I can't let it bother me.

—Reliever Dennis Cook, from *Indians on the Game* by Wayne Stewart

I didn't know much. I just reared back and let them go . . . Sometimes I threw the ball clean up into the stands.

—Hall of Famer Bob Feller of his early days with Cleveland

A stadium with the lights out.

—Pitcher Charlie Hough, when asked what would constitute perfect conditions for a knuckleball pitcher like himself

I threw so hard I thought my arm would fly right off my body.

—Pitching great Smoky Joe Wood

How many 20-game seasons has Jesse Owens got?

—Pitcher Luis Tiant on his attitude about pitchers having to run sprints

An effective relief pitcher has to have ice water in his veins.

—Dodgers manager Walt Alston

Not when you're 1–6. I learned it from Lindy McDaniel, but I learned it from watching, not talking to him about it. I changed speeds on it and used it as a good off-speed pitch.

—Hall of Famer Gaylord Perry on the difficulty of learning, and the throwing of, his spitball, from *Pitching Secrets of the Pros* by Wayne Stewart

That son of a bitch is so mean, he'd [expletive] knock you down in the dugout.

—Outfielder Mickey Mantle on Early Wynn

Let them think I throw it [the spitball]. That gives me an edge because it's another pitch they have to worry about.

—Pitcher Lew Burdette

When a pitcher's in a groove, or in the zone, every pitch you throw, you know where it's going—you know what location it's going to. It seems like it's automatic, the ball's going to go there—but that only happens once in a while.

—Reliever Justin Speier, from *Indians on the Game* by Wayne Stewart

When I started to throw the ball back to the pitcher harder than he was throwing to me, we changed positions.

—All-time great Bert Blyleven on when he became a pitcher

Watching him pitch is like a struggling artist watching Michelangelo paint.

—Pitcher Jerry Reuss on Tom Seaver

[Steve] Carlton does not pitch to the hitter, he pitches through him. The batter hardly exists for Steve. He's playing an elevated game of catch.

—Carlton's catcher Tim McCarver

I know they're loaded. Did you think I thought they gave me an extra infield?

—Yankees pitching great Lefty Gomez, when told to bear down because the bases were loaded, from *Baseball Is a Funny Game* by Joe Garagiola

Ryne Duren was a one-pitch pitcher. His one pitch was a wild [intimidating] warm-up.

—Pitcher Jim Bouton on the blazing hard, and wild, pitching of Duren

When [Rube] Waddell had control—and some sleep—he was unbeatable.

—Team executive Branch Rickey

Newk [Don Newcombe], you better do somethin', because when I signal for the express you throws me the local.

—Catcher Roy Campanella

We've gotten in brawls with him in the past. Then he usually runs and hides in the dugout. . . . [Pitching up around batters' faces] may be a way to keep guys off edge, and you can do it, but it's certainly not going to make you any friends on the other teams.

—Indians pitcher Paul Shuey on Pedro Martinez

The only way that shot would have stayed in the ballpark is if it hit the Goodyear blimp.

—Dodgers pitcher Tom Niedenfuer on the 1985 NLCS-clinching homer he surrendered to Jack Clark

I think too much on the mound sometimes and I get brain cramps.

—Pitcher Britt Burns

If that starts to happen [fame going to his head], I want somebody on the club to smack me. I want somebody to say, "You're too cocky. You're not that good. You're only a rookie."

—Detroit pitcher Mark "the Bird" Fidrych

[Eddie] Lopat looks like he is throwing wads of tissue paper. Every time he wins a game, fans come down out of the stands asking for contracts.

—Yankees manager Casey Stengel on his junkball pitcher

Since I don't have one, the only thing I have to fear is fear itself.

—Reliever Dan Quisenberry, when asked if he feared losing his fastball

John [Wetteland] gives us the confidence that if we can win the first eight innings, we'll win the game 99 percent of the time.

—Texas pitcher John Burkett on his teammate, from *The History of the Texas Rangers* by Aaron Frisch

He could throw a cream puff through a battleship.

—Brooklyn's Johnny Frederick on pitcher Dazzy Vance (also listed as throwing a "soft-boiled egg through a battleship," and attributed to writer Blackie Sherrod on Don Drysdale)

In my early years I never learned to "pitch," because I didn't think I had to. I figured that even if I walked a few batters, I could power pitch my way out of a jam. . . . [Later] I realized I had to be a "pitcher" out there, not just a thrower.

—Hall of Fame pitcher Bob Feller, from *Baseball for the Love of It* by Anthony J. Connor

You've got to be lucky, but if you have good stuff, it's easier to be lucky.

—Pitcher Sandy Koufax on throwing no-hitters

It's like a butterfly with hiccups. If you don't have a long flyswatter, you're in trouble.

—Pirates outfielder Willie Stargell on knuckleballs

Stalling won't help. There's one more out to go and you're it.

—Indians pitcher Dennis Eckersley to the final out of his no-hitter, Angels batter Gil Flores

I don't want to see the hits going past me.

—Dodger pitcher Fernando Valenzuela on why he gazes up in the sky as he pitches

A lot of guys can win, but can't win 1–0 games.

—Cleveland's stellar pitcher Bob Feller, from *Indians on the Game* by Wayne Stewart

[Warren] Spahn did not win his first major league game until . . . the age of twenty-five. But once he began winning, he simply did not stop.

—Lawrence Ritter and Donald Honig of 363-game winner Spahn, from their *The Image of Their Greatness*

All pitchers are liars and crybabies.

—Catcher Yogi Berra

It's nice pitching in an airport.

—Pitcher Vida Blue on his home park, the Oakland Coliseum

Go out there and pitch three innings or four hours, whichever comes first.

—Pirates manager Danny Murtaugh to deliberate-pitching Steve Blass

[Against Nolan Ryan] you just hoped to mix in a walk so you could have a good night and go 0-for-3.

—Outfielder Reggie Jackson

You all done? You comfortable? Well, send for the groundskeeper and get a shovel because that's where they're gonna bury you.

—Pitcher Dizzy Dean to an opposing batter who had dug himself in at the plate

CHAPTER FOUR

Stars and Superstars

Here you will find some of the words spoken by and about the true superstars of the game, as well as men who are lesser stars, but legitimately fine players nevertheless.

I've interviewed players since 1978 and found that frequently the most willing subjects and often the most interesting ones are not the stars, but marginal players. However, that said, some of my favorite interviewees were astute, incisive, and articulate men, such as Tony Gwynn, Doug Drabek, Merv Rettenmund, Lee Smith, and Dale Murphy, all of them stars or superstars by anyone's definition.

So, while great quotations *can* come from virtually any baseball player, it's also true that most fans would much rather hear what the big stars have to say. When Vida Blue was a rookie back in 1971, he burst upon the baseball scene with the speed and force of a meteor. It didn't take him long to catch on to the fickle ways of the world. As he summed up, "It's a weird scene. You win a few baseball games and all of a sudden you're surrounded by reporters and TV men with cameras asking you about Vietnam and race relations."

Pete Rose, not a huge man, but one whose bulging forearms begged not for a tattoo of a battleship, but of an entire armada, is far from being a well-educated man, but when the subject is baseball, people pay heed—and that's quite natural. So natural that we've devoted an entire chapter to comments from the mouths of the game's luminaries. Not all of the quotations are exactly earth shattering, but hopefully they are of note.

The rostrum is loaded with men such as Ted Williams and Ty Cobb, fierce .400 hitters; Hank Aaron and Reggie Jackson, both laden with power; men from as far back as "Shoeless Joe" Jackson and players as recent as Johnny Damon.

So it's time now to listen to the words of and about men with split-second

timing with the bat and precise hand-eye coordination. These are the men who made a name for themselves in the world of baseball, the stars and the superstars.

I don't care to be known as a .400 hitter with a lousy average of .39955.

—Boston legend Ted Williams on his refusal to sit out a season-ending doubleheader to preserve his mathematically rounded-up-to-.400 average in 1941

I had to be first all the time—first in everything. All I ever thought about was winning.

—Detroit's Ty Cobb

I used more effort winding up than he did in pitching nine innings.

—Pitcher Burleigh Grimes in awe of Grover Cleveland Alexander

When I hit two home runs [in one game early in his career] . . . one of them after my top hand slipped off the bat—it started everybody talking about home runs and when people around the Negro League talked about home runs, they talked about Josh Gibson.

—Slugger Hank Aaron, from *I Had a Hammer* by Aaron with Lonnie Wheeler

This game was invented for Willie Mays a hundred years ago.

—Pitcher Ray Sadecki, from *The Red Smith Reader*, edited by Dave Anderson, also attributed to Ted Williams

When he [Rickey Henderson] came around, there wasn't anybody like him. He definitely was a trendsetter and he's what teams are looking for in a leadoff hitter. Before [him], leadoff hitters were just slap hitters and guys who could run very fast, but Rickey added the power to that game.

—Outfielder Johnny Damon, from *Hitting Secrets of the Pros* by Wayne Stewart

He's the kind of guy you'd like to kill if he's playing for the other team, but you'd take ten of him on your side.

—General manager Frank Lane on Billy Martin

He [Babe Ruth] said he thought [Ty] Cobb was a great ballplayer but a no-good, mean sonofabitch. Babe wasn't alone on that. Ninety percent of the players felt the same way. Cobb was very much hated.

—Quote from writer Fred Lieb, from *No Cheering in the Press Box*, recorded and edited by Jerome Holtzman

It was nothing for me to hit two home runs and punch out three times. That was a "Reggie" day—a hat trick and a couple of bombs.
—Slugger Reggie Jackson

If he stays healthy, I guarantee he'll be making a [Hall of Fame] acceptance speech someday.
—Texas manager Johnny Oates of a young Ivan Rodriguez, from *The History of the Texas Rangers* by Aaron Frisch

[Ty] Cobb is about as welcome in American League parks as a rattlesnake.
—Hall of Famer Lou Gehrig

I got hit enough times to have [baseball commissioner] Ford Frick's signature tattooed on my arms and body.
—Outfielder Enos Slaughter

For me, it was a lousy year.

—Cardinals great Stan Musial to a man who had just apologized to him for having earlier labeled Musial's .312, 95 RBI season in 1947 "a lousy year," from *Red Smith on Baseball* compiled by Phyllis W. Smith

He could probably hit a ball harder in every direction than any man who ever played. Lou could hit hard line drives past an outfielder the way I hit hard line drives past an infielder.

—Yankees catcher Bill Dickey on teammate Lou Gehrig, from *The History of the New York Yankees* by Richard Rambeck

Stealing bases is like jumping out of a car that's going twenty miles per hour.

—Speedster Willie Wilson of the Royals

If you took those two legs and barbecued them, you'd have enough to feed a family for a month.

—Shortstop Larry Bowa on big Greg Luzinski

The screwball's an unnatural pitch. Nature never intended a man to turn his hand like that throwing rocks at a bear.

—Carl Hubbell of his patented pitch

He is the only baseball player I know who is a bigger hero to his teammates than he is to the fans.

—Yankees third baseman Clete Boyer on Mickey Mantle

I've got a hitch in my swing and I hit off the wrong foot. I've done it the wrong way my whole career.

—Braves immortal Hank Aaron

What I don't understand is why you ask where I've gone. I just did a Mr. Coffee commercial, I'm a spokesman for the Bowery Savings Bank, and I haven't gone anywhere.

—Yankees star Joe DiMaggio alluding to the lyrics of the song "Mrs. Robinson"

I always say, the only time you gotta worry about getting booed is when you're wearing a white [home] uniform. And I've never been booed wearing a white uniform.

—Batting champ Pete Rose, from *The Philadelphia Inquirer* (story by Rose), reprinted in the *Complete Armchair Book of Baseball*, edited by John Thorn

You are my center fielder. Today. Tomorrow. For as long as I'm managing this club. I'm not sending you back down [to the minors]. You are my center fielder.

—Giants manager Leo Durocher to a diffident rookie, Willie Mays, from *The Era* by Roger Kahn

Maybe they should see if his body is corked.

—Third baseman Howard Johnson on powerful Bo Jackson, from *Sports Illustrated*

[Mickey] Mantle is the only man I ever saw who was crippled who could outdo the world.

—Manager Casey Stengel

If I played in New York, they'd name a candy bar after me.

—Slugger Reggie Jackson

Does Pete [Rose] hustle? Before the All-Star Game he came into the clubhouse and took off his shoes—and they ran another mile without him.

—All-time great Hank Aaron

Ain't no man can avoid being born average, but there ain't no man got to be common.

—Star pitcher Satchel Paige

If they throw too hard, I'll take one [get hit by a pitch] for the team. If you can't hit them, let them hit you.

—Infielder Ron Hunt, former record holder for the most times hit by a pitch

When Joe [DiMaggio] came into the clubhouse it was like a senator or a president coming in.

—Yankees infielder Billy Martin

I have a darn good job with the Cardinals, but please don't ask me what I do.
—Hall of Famer Stan Musial

He'd run the bases with his head down as if he was embarrassed for the pitcher.
—David Mantle on his father's class after homering

He was gamer than a dentist pulling his own teeth . . . But he was as touchy as fingerprint powder and would climb a mountain to take a punch at an echo.
—Sportswriter Arthur Baer on Ty Cobb

He looked like he was falling apart when he ran. Looked like he was coming apart when he threw. His stance at the plate was ridiculous . . . The only thing that made him look sensational was the results.
—Pitcher Robin Roberts on Roberto Clemente

I've been calling big-league games for forty years and I can't remember anybody capturing the imaginations of the fans quite like this kid.
—Cubs announcer Harry Caray on Ryne Sandberg

Joe [McCarthy], I'm out of the lineup. I'm just not doing the team any good.

—Yankees great Lou Gehrig, taking himself out of the lineup, thus ending his streak of 2,130 consecutive games played

Take Ted Williams—after all he did to the fans in Boston. He spat on them, gave them the obscene and vulgar gesture and, Christ, he hits a home run and they all stand up and cheer. You can't boo a home run.

—Quote from writer Shirley Povich, from *No Cheering in the Press Box,* recorded and edited by Jerome Holtzman

Robin [Yount] had so much ability, we just had to let him play. He was just a baby out there, but you could see early on that he'd be a great one.

—Yount's first big-league manager, Del Crandall, from *The History of the Milwaukee Brewers* by Richard Rambeck

Bobo Newsom always held out just for exercise [to avoid it]. He hated spring training.

—Sportswriter Furman Bisher

[Lou] Gehrig never learned that a ballplayer couldn't be good every day.

—Catcher Hank Gowdy

Big Papi [David Ortiz] is an action superhero come to life.

—*Boston Globe* writer Dan Shaughnessy, from *Baseball Digest*, December 2006

Back when I came up, baseball was about establishing yourself. You wanted to get into a position to break the records of the players you grew up watching.

—Padres hitting sensation Tony Gwynn

The big trouble is not really who isn't in the Hall of Fame, but who is. It was established for a select few.

—Hall of Famer Rogers Hornsby

I don't want to be a star. Stars get blamed too much.

—Fifteen-year veteran Enos Cabell

When baseball is no longer fun, it's no longer a game. . . . And so, I have played my last game of ball.

—Yankees star Joe DiMaggio, announcing his retirement, from *Red Smith on Baseball*, compiled by Phyllis W. Smith

If the game becomes more namby-pamby, they may have to put the ball on a batting tee.

—Pitcher Don Drysdale

When Ty's southern blood is aroused he is a bad man to handle.

—Manager Hughie Jennings on Cobb

When Henry came up, I heard the fans yell, "Hit that [n-word]! Hit that [n-word]." Henry hit the ball up against the clock. The next time he came up, they said, "Walk him, walk him."

—Herbert Aaron, Henry's father, from *www.webcircle.com*

They hung the nickname "the Commerce Comet" on him, except he was faster than a comet. Fastest thing I ever saw.

—Yankees pitcher Tom Sturdivant on Mickey Mantle

He [track star Carl Lewis] makes his living running fast and I make mine running slow.

—Power hitter Barry Bonds on his deliberate home run trot

Before the game they told me I looked like Babe Ruth. Then, in my bat against Don Carman, I looked like Dr. Ruth.

—Outfielder John Kruk

I guess this is one of the few times when you get to see your own last rites.

—Pitcher Steve Stone upon his retirement

Your body is just like a bar of soap. It gradually wears down from repeated use.

—Power hitter Dick Allen

Prospects are a dime a dozen.

—Oakland A's owner Charlie Finley

I get $1,000 for every old-timer game. By playing seven times a year, I make as much playing baseball as I did in 1951 as a rookie.

—Minnie Minoso, 1990

It took fifteen years to get you out of a game. Sometimes I'm out in fifteen minutes.

—Pitcher Lefty Gomez to Lou Gehrig

You look at the Braves media guide and you need almost a day to look through [Hank Aaron's records]. A lot of people don't realize that he's third [for] all-time hits because of all the other things that he did. He was awesome.

—Hitting coach Gerald Perry

One time in the car I asked him [Hank Aaron] why he never talked about hitting . . . I'll never forget what he said. He said, "If you can do it, you don't have to talk about it."

—Braves publicity director Bob Allen, from *I Had a Hammer* by Hank Aaron with Lonnie Wheeler

It ain't what it was, but then what the hell is?

—Pitcher Dizzy Dean on his arm as he grew older

The boy's got talent and desire, but he ain't got no neck.

—Manager John McGraw on Hack Wilson

More has been written about the colorful Willie Mays in one year than was said of [Arky] Vaughan in a lifetime.

—Sportswriter Arthur Daley, from *The Bill James Historical Baseball Abstract* by Bill James

Derek Jeter is a great player. He didn't have to prove it this [2000] Series. He could have taken it off and I still would have thought he was a great player.

—Mets manager Bobby Valentine

He was the best one-legged player I ever saw play the game.

—Manager Casey Stengel on the hobbled Mickey Mantle

Thinking about the things that happened, I don't know any other ballplayer who could have done what he did [break the "color barrier" in baseball].

—Dodgers star Pee Wee Reese on teammate Jackie Robinson

He made two mistakes. The first was a slider that didn't slide. The second was a curve that didn't curve.

—Richie Zisk, Pirates outfielder

Everybody in the park knows he's going to run [steal] and he makes it anyway.

—Shortstop Larry Bowa on Lou Brock

When the pressure builds up, it's like being on a bus in a mudhole. The harder you press on the pedal, the further you sink in the mud.

—Yankees star Bob Watson

He plays hurt, he plays hard, and he comes to beat the other team. That's a manager's dream.

—Jim Leyland, Tigers manager in 2006 on his catcher Ivan Rodriguez

When Steve [Carlton] and I die, we are going to be buried in the same cemetery, sixty feet, six inches apart.

—Catcher Tim McCarver on his batterymate

Just as nature fills a vacuum, Reggie [Jackson] fills a spotlight.

—Author Bob Marshall

Batting against Don Drysdale is the same as making a date with the dentist.

—Shortstop Dick Groat

[Lou] Gehrig was a very straightforward honest guy. Once he did an advertising spiel for corn flakes and at the end of the spiel they asked him, "And, Lou, what is your favorite breakfast food?" He answers, "Wheaties."

—Sportswriter John Drebinger, from *No Cheering in the Press Box*, recorded and edited by Jerome Holtzman

The place [Montreal] was always cold and I got the feeling that the fans would have enjoyed baseball more if it had been played with a hockey puck.

—Outfielder Andre Dawson

Tonight, I stand here overwhelmed, as my name is linked with the great and courageous Lou Gehrig. I am truly humbled to have our names spoken in the same breath.

—Ironman Cal Ripken, Jr. upon breaking Gehrig's consecutive games played record

This team, it all flows from me. I've got to keep it going. I'm the straw that stirs the drink.

—Yankee Reggie Jackson

There were days when Mickey Mantle was so darn good that we kids would bet that even God would want his autograph.

—Announcer Bob Costas

I don't think the fires ever went out in him, not till the day he died.

—All-Star infielder Ossie Bluege on Ty Cobb

He [Don Baylor] was like God in the Yankees clubhouse. When you did wrong, he went in there and balled you out—you had to listen to him because he knew what he was talking about. He was like a cop, he took care of the guys.

—Charles Zabransky, retired Yankees clubhouse attendant

We're a bunch of battlers, except for Frank [Thomas]. He's a big battler. He's the mother of battleships.

—Oakland's Nick Swisher on his slugging teammate in 2006

[Willie] Wilson has unreal speed. He's a walking double.

—Outfielder Reggie Jackson

You grab hold of him and it's like grabbing hold of steel.

—Cubs manager Bob Scheffing on his star player Ernie Banks

I'm no different from anyone else with two legs and 4,200 hits.

—Hit king Pete Rose

Cal's retirement brings an end to one of the finest, most noble careers this game has ever seen.

—Orioles great Brooks Robinson on Cal Ripken Jr., from *The History of the Baltimore Orioles* by John Nichols

If I can change the score, I'm not going to worry about getting hurt.

—Aggressive baserunner Pete Rose

They [modern players] are entitled to it [large salaries] and I am all for it. In fact, it is a changing world for the old-timers, too. I make more money now traveling around the country and appearing at card shows with hobby groups than I ever made as a player.

—Hall of Famer Bob Feller

When there's runners in scoring position, you almost see him switch modes into his automatic run-producer. It's special to watch.

—Mets third baseman David Wright on slugger Carlos Delgado, 2006

If you want to be a great hitter, don't go to the movies—it ruins your eyes.

—Hall of Famer Rogers Hornsby

Even now I look up to him; he's never disappointed me.

—Outfielder Andy Pafko on Joe DiMaggio

He is the one player in our league who could win the pennant for any of the seven teams that were not in first place.

—Umpire Bill Klem on pitcher Grover Cleveland Alexander, from the Baseball Hall of Fame website

Making the majors is not as hard as staying there, staying interested day after day. It's like being married. The hardest part is to stay married.

—Braves legend Hank Aaron

They say you have to be good to be lucky, but I think you have to be lucky to be good.

—Outfielder/designated hitter Rico Carty

[Greg Maddux's] kind of talent usually comes with an ego sidecar. He doesn't have it. He's as easygoing as the guy next door.

—Braves general manager John Schuerholz

This man [Jackie Robinson] turned a stumbling block into a stepping stone.

—Reverend Jesse Jackson

And now Boston knows how England felt when it lost India.

—Author Ed Linn on Ted Williams' retirement, from "The Kid's Last Game" by Ed Linn in *Sport* Magazine, reprinted in *The Baseball Reader* by Charles Einstein

Bob [Gibson] wasn't just unfriendly when he pitched. I'd say it was more like hateful.

—Former catcher Joe Torre

I don't think anybody has ever been that good at that age [19]. He's in his own category.

—Mariners hitting coach Gene Clines on Ken Griffey Jr., from *The History of the Seattle Mariners* by Michael E. Goodman

We have three leagues now. There's the American, the National, and there's Ted Williams.

—Red Sox pitcher Mickey Harris

The financial careers of most professional athletes can be summed up in these words: short and sweet—but mostly short.

—Giants great Willie Mays

This game is too much fun to ever get too old to play it.

—Pitcher Tug McGraw

It will be a great honor if I'm voted in, but it's something a player should never expect will happen.

—Hall of Famer Warren Spahn

I have the greatest job in the world.

—Yankees shortstop Derek Jeter

There's no scouting report on handling Albert Pujols. "Don't even try," the [unnamed] scout says.

—Quote from *USA Today* prior to 2006 playoffs

He could have hit .300 with a fountain pen.

—Sportscaster Joe Garagiola on Stan Musial

When I played ball, I didn't play for fun. To me it wasn't parchesi played under parchesi rules. Baseball is a red-blooded sport for red-blooded men. It's no pink team and mollycoddles had better stay out.

—Charter member of the Hall of Fame, Ty Cobb

I can tell you Billy [Martin] has a great heart, but I can't vouch for his liver.

—Pitcher Whitey Ford

The planes at LaGuardia had better not fly too low when I'm at bat.

—Slugger George Foster

He had lightnin' on the ball.

—Manager Casey Stengel on Bob Meusel

Show me a guy who's afraid to look bad and I'll show you a guy you can beat every time.

—Hall of Famer Lou Brock

If my uniform doesn't get dirty, I haven't done anything in the baseball game.

—Star outfielder Rickey Henderson

Because I wanted to win the game.

—Outfielder Roger Maris, when asked why he bunted rather than went for the fences

I'm not sure I know what the hell charisma is, but I get the feeling it's Willie Mays.

—Slugger Ted Kluszewski

To play ball was all I lived for.

—Yankee outfielder Mickey Mantle

I've found that you don't need to wear a necktie if you can hit.

—Boston great Ted Williams

The day I got a hit off [Sandy] Koufax was when he knew it was over.

—Sparky Anderson of his light-hitting days with the Phillies

He can't hit, he can't run, he can't throw—all he can do is beat you.

—Manager Leo Durocher on scrappy Eddie Stanky

You have to love talent, baby and I have nothing but talent. Why, I amaze myself.

—First baseman/outfielder Ken Harrelson

I wasn't going to walk him. That wouldn't have been fair to him or me. Hell, he's the greatest player I ever saw.

—St. Louis Browns pitcher Bob Muncrief, who had the chance to stop Joe DiMaggio's hitting streak at 35, but challenged him and surrendered a single in DiMaggio's last at-bat of the game

I'd walk into the owner's office to talk contract and I'd say, "Hi ya, partner."

—Yankees great Joe DiMaggio, when asked what he'd be worth in the era of free agency

Brooks [Robinson] never asked anyone to name a candy bar after him. In Baltimore, people name their children after him.

—Sportswriter Gordon Beard

A foul ball was a moral victory.

—Pitcher Don Sutton on Sandy Koufax

Too many people think an athlete's life can be an open book. You're supposed to be an example. Why do I have to be an example for your kid? You be an example for your kid.

—Pitching ace Bob Gibson

It's like crying for your mother after she's gone. You cry because you love her. I cried, I guess, because I loved baseball and I knew I had to leave it.

—All-time great Willie Mays, then with the Mets

Son, what kind of a pitch would you like to miss?

—Pitcher Dizzy Dean to a batter

During my 18 years I came to bat almost 10,000 times. I struck out about 1,700 times and walked maybe 1,800 times. You figure a ballplayer will average about 500 at-bats a season. That means I played seven years in the major leagues without even hitting the ball.

—Yankees great Mickey Mantle

Throw the ball three feet over his head and outside and he'll hit it down the left field line. Three feet over his head and inside and he'll go to right.

—Pitcher Pat Zachry on bad-ball hitter Jose Cruz, from *The History of the Houston Astros* by Michael E. Goodman

I really thought they [Stan Musial, Ted Williams, and Jackie Robinson] put their pants on different, rather than one leg at a time.

—Superstar Hank Aaron

I ain't never had a job. I just always played baseball.

—Pitcher Satchel Paige

He could do the five things you have to do to be a superstar: hit, hit with power, run, throw, and field. And he had that other magic ingredient that turns a superstar into a super superstar. He lit up the room when he came in.

—Giants manager Leo Durocher on Willie Mays

I thought I might become Rice-A-Roni.

—Pitcher Jim Colborn after strongman Jim Rice charged the mound

Anyone can light it up for one or two starts. To do it over the course of a year, you have to be a superstar.

—Manager Joe Torre on Roger Clemens

He learned in one or two years what it took me ten years to learn. He uses the whole field, foul line to foul line.

—Seattle's Edgar Martinez on a young Alex Rodriguez, from *www.baseballalmanac.com*

If the human body recognized agony and frustration, people would never run marathons, have babies, or play baseball.

—Catcher Carlton Fisk

No matter how many errors you make, no matter how many times you strike out, keep hustling. That way you'll at least look like a ballplayer.

—Yankees star shortstop Tony Kubek

Here stands baseball's perfect warrior. Here stands baseball's perfect knight.

—Baseball commissioner Ford Frick on St. Louis superstar Stan Musial

I ain't afraid to tell the world that it don't take school stuff to help a fella play ball.

—White Sox standout "Shoeless Joe" Jackson

He was sometimes unbearable, but he was never dull.

—Biographer Ed Linn on Ted Williams

The ballplayer who loses his head, who can't keep his cool, is worse than no ballplayer at all.

—Yankees legend Lou Gehrig

I'd rather swing a bat than do anything else in the world.

—Boston superstar Ted Williams

Babe Ruth will always be number one. Before I broke his [lifetime home run] record it was the greatest of all. Then I broke it and suddenly the greatest record is Joe DiMaggio's hitting streak.

—Slugger Hank Aaron

You don't think Hemingway or Michelangelo would have been delighted to see their achievements surpassed, do you?

—Speedster Maury Wills when Lou Brock topped his record for stolen bases in a season

With the money I'm making, I should be playing two positions.

—Versatile Pete Rose, with the Phillies

I'd had it and this was the end. . . . It flashed through my mind, "This guy thinks he can throw it past me." Next time he threw, I was swinging.

—Boston great Ted Williams on his home run off Jack Fisher in the final at-bat of his career

Maybe I'm not a great man, but I damn well want to break the record.

—Yankees outfielder Roger Maris on topping Babe Ruth's single-season home run mark

Home run hitters drive Cadillacs. Singles hitters drive Fords.

—Slugger Ralph Kiner

People ask me what I do in winter when there's no baseball. I'll tell you what I do. I stare out the window and wait for spring.

—Hall of Famer Rogers Hornsby

[Willie] Wilson may be the fastest person I've seen in a uniform.

—Wilson's Kansas City manager Whitey Herzog

Money and women. They're the two strongest things in the world. The things you do for a woman you wouldn't do for anything else. Same with money.

—Negro Leagues star Satchel Paige

He once hit a ball between my legs so hard that my center fielder caught it on the fly backing up against the wall.

—Pitcher Dizzy Dean on hard-hitting Bill Terry of the Giants

When you're hitting the ball, it comes at you looking like a grapefruit. When you're not, it looks like a black-eyed pea.

—First baseman George Scott

No other left-hander gave me so much trouble. When I think about how many points of Earl Averill's lifetime average came off Gomez deliveries, I thank the good Lord he wasn't twins. One more like him would probably have kept me out of the Hall of Fame.

—Pitcher Lefty Gomez, from the Baseball Hall of Fame website

I'm tired of hearing all those stories that I'd throw at my mother . . . unless she had a bat in her hands.

—Hall of Fame pitcher Early Wynn

If I was being paid $30,000 a year, the very least I could do was hit .400.

—Outfielder Ted Williams

He's a terrific guy and the world's quietest person. The night he broke [Lou] Gehrig's record, he went out and painted the town beige.

—Billy Ripken, utility man, on his brother Cal, also attributed to Vin Scully, speaking about the quiet, reserved Burt Hooton

The whole secret of sliding is to make your move at the last possible second. When I went in there I wanted to see the whites of the fielder's eyes.

—Tigers superstar Ty Cobb

[Joe] DiMaggio's streak is the most extraordinary thing that ever happened in American sports.

—Writer Stephen Jay Gould

When you're eight games behind, it's like eight miles; when you're eight games in front, it's like eight inches.

—Cubs star third baseman Ron Santo, from *www.webcircle.com*

You must have an alibi to show why you lost. If you haven't one, you must fake one. Your self-confidence must be maintained. Always have an alibi. But keep it to yourself. That's where it belongs.

—Christy Mathewson, pitching great

I'd rather be a swingman on a championship team than a regular on another team.

—Outfielder Lou Piniella as a Yankee

Nobody who ever put on a uniform ever played the game harder than Rose. He could beat you in so many ways, it was unbelievable. He simply knew how to win.

—Reds manager Sparky Anderson on Cincinnati star Pete Rose, from *Baseball Digest*, May 2003

I had a speech ready but somewhere along in 28 years it got lost.

—A bitter Johnny Mize, finally inducted into the Hall of Fame in 1981

When I'm really struggling, I have to try easier. Everybody always says you have to try harder; in baseball, if you try harder, you tense up, you put too much pressure on yourself. The key is to just back off, take a deep breath, and try easier.

—Indians announcer Matt Underwood, quoting slugger Matt Williams, from *Indians on the Game* by Wayne Stewart

The kid can't play baseball. He can't pull the ball.

—Minor league manager Tommy Holmes going 0-for-2 as a prognosticator regarding a young Hank Aaron

He's so good, I even worry about him in the winter.

—Slugger Ted Williams on pitcher Bob Lemon

You look for his weakness and while you're looking for it, he's liable to hit 45 home runs.

—Pitcher Satchel Paige on Josh Gibson

I never perceived myself to be the big star. I'm only one of nine guys. I think it is good to think that way.

—Baltimore legend Cal Ripken Jr.

D.H.-ing itself is not the thing that bothers me, it's the length of time between at bats. It makes me respect bench players. You get an at bat and might not get another chance to hit for forty minutes. You've got to keep loose because you're not in the game.

—Slugger Jim Thome, the *Plain Dealer*, September 15, 2000

Every time I look at my pocketbook, I see Jackie Robinson.

—Hall of Famer Willie Mays

There are certain people in American sports who are now valid figures in the nation's history books. Jackie Robinson is one.

—Announcer Howard Cosell

The games were the easy part. Those hours were the only times when I got any relief from the pressure.

—Outfielder Roger Maris on his record-setting (61 homers) 1961 season

The hardest part of any slump is looking up at the scoreboard and seeing your stats in huge numbers.

—A's and Yankees star Jason Giambi

I loved the game. I loved the competition. But I never had any fun. I never enjoyed it. All hard work, all the time.

—Boston great Carl Yastrzemski

He hit a popup against us one day that went so high, all nine guys on our team called for it.

—Rich Donnelly, Marlins coach, on Mark McGwire

I may not have been the greatest pitcher ever, but I was amongst ’em.

—St. Louis legend Dizzy Dean

I’ll kill anybody that gets in my way.

—Fiery outfielder Ty Cobb

There’s no pressure here. This is a lot of fun. Pressure is when you have to go to the unemployment office to pick up a check to support four people.

—Royals star George Brett

A ballplayer’s got to be kept hungry to become a big leaguer. That’s why no boy from a rich family ever made the big leagues.

—Outfielder Joe DiMaggio

Playing baseball for a living is like having a license to steal.

—Reds superstar Pete Rose

The best movement on his fastball is Pedro Martinez. I think the best breaking ball is probably Pedro Martinez and I think the best straight changeup I've ever seen is Pedro Martinez. So, safe to say, I think he's the best pitcher I've ever seen.

—All-Star Travis Fryman

I've only known three or four perfect swings in baseball. This kid has one of them.

—Ty Cobb on Braves star third baseman Eddie Mathews

I play my six-year-old daughter in tic-tac-toe and beat her brains out.

—Highly competitive pitcher Bob Gibson

There's only one difference between a game in May and a game in September. You lose in September, there's less time to get it back.

—Pirates superstar Roberto Clemente

The best way to pitch Stan Musial? That's easy—walk him and then try to pick him off first base.

—Catcher Joe Garagiola

You can only milk a cow so long, then you're left holding the pail.

—Superstar Hank Aaron on his retirement

He was asked to be a leader at twenty-one. You'd have to ask Gandhi to handle some of the pressure Dave's had and Gandhi couldn't have pitched for the Toronto Blue Jays.

—Agent Bob LaMonte on his client, pitcher Dave Steib, from *The History of the Toronto Blue Jays* by Richard Rambeck

I'm not sure which is more insulting, being offered in a trade or having it turned down.

—Star pitcher Claude Osteen

He is Cincinnati. He's the Reds.

—Reds manager Sparky Anderson on Pete Rose

He's the nearest thing to a perfect ballplayer.

—Baseball legend Ty Cobb on Hall of Famer George Sisler

Whenever I caught against him he'd step up to the plate and ask me about my family. But before I could answer he'd be on third base.

—Joe Garagiola on Hall of Famer Stan Musial, from *Baseball's Funniest People* by Michael J. Pellowski

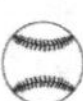

One year I hit .291 and had to take a salary cut. If you hit .291 today, you'd own the franchise.

—Cardinals star Enos Slaughter

Pete Rose is the most likable arrogant person I've ever met.

—Phillies great Mike Schmidt

I wound up, threw, and then ducked behind the mound.

—Pitcher Walter Masterson on throwing to Ted Williams

I want to thank the good Lord for making me a Yankee.

—Center fielder Joe DiMaggio

If a tie is like kissing your sister, losing is like kissing your grandmother with her teeth out.

—George Brett, Hall of Fame third baseman

He's the motor that makes us go. He contributes as much to this team as any man and pound-for-pound he's the best player in the game.

—Cincinnati manager Sparky Anderson on his star second baseman Joe Morgan, from *Baseball Digest*, May 2003

When I'm 40 years old, I'd still like to be able to comb my hair.

—Dodger great pitcher Sandy Koufax on why he was retiring early

They used to say, "If we find a good black player, we'll sign him." They was lying.

—Negro Leagues sensation Cool Papa Bell

Hitting the ball was easy. Running around the bases was the tough part.

—Yankees outfielder Mickey Mantle

[Greg] Maddux just never gives you anything to hit. He just keeps changing speeds and painting the corners. It makes for a long day.

—Tony Gwynn, San Diego star outfielder

He's out there to have fun. That eases a lot of the pressure. The best thing about him is that he doesn't take himself too seriously, not like a lot of the superstars.

—Pitcher Andy Hassler of Royals teammate George Brett, from *The History of the Kansas City Royals* by Richard Rambeck

Some of us shake on the outside, some of us on the inside.

—Pirates superstar Roberto Clemente

Pitchers did me a favor when they knocked me down. It made me more determined. I wouldn't let that pitcher get me out. They say you can't hit if you're on your back, but I didn't hit on my back—I got up.

—Hall of Famer Frank Robinson

I don't think baseball has a superstar today, regardless of what the salaries say. Henry Aaron, Willie Mays, Joe DiMaggio were superstars.

—Hall of Famer Willie McCovey in 1978

You could stack it up and a show dog couldn't jump over it.

—Superstar Pete Rose on what his multimillion-dollar salary would look like if placed in a pile

I want to be remembered as a ballplayer who gave all he had to give.

—Pirates great Roberto Clemente

I think DiMaggio was underestimated as a player. He did things so easily, [that] people didn't realize how good he was. DiMaggio would hit a home run, but nobody would get excited. He could do so many things to keep the other team from beating you.

—Yankees catcher Bill Dickey on Hall of Fame outfielder Joe DiMaggio from *The History of the New York Yankees* by Richard Rambeck

In Cincinnati once I hit the left-field wall and they threw me out at first.

—Hall of Famer Ernie Lombardi, a notoriously slow runner

The only change is that baseball has turned Paige from a second-class citizen to a second-class immortal.

—Pitcher Satchel Paige on being inducted into the Hall of Fame

His trouble is he takes life too seriously. [Ty] Cobb is going at it too hard.

—Pitching great Cy Young

The Hall of Fame is for baseball people. Heaven is for good people.

—Outfielder Jim Dwyer, contending Pete Rose deserves induction into the hall

A champion is one who can't settle for second best.

—Superstar pitcher Warren Spahn

Most guys hit when they can; he hits when he wants.

—Former teammate Gary Pettis on Carew

Either he throws the fastest ball I've ever seen, or I'm going blind.

—Outfielder Richie Ashburn on Sandy Koufax

Slapping a rattlesnake across the face with the back of your hand is safer than trying to fool Henry Aaron.

—Pitcher Claude Osteen

It's tomorrow that counts. So you worry all the time. It never ends. Lord, baseball is a worrying thing.

—Pitcher Stan Coveleski

He's better than one of the best. He is the best.

—Atlanta Braves manager Bobby Cox on Colorado star Larry Walker, c. 2000

I'll never be considered one of the all-time greats, maybe not even one of the all-time goods, but I'm one of the all-time survivors.

—Jim Kaat, 25-year big-league pitcher

He [Joe DiMaggio] had the greatest instinct of any ballplayer I ever saw. He made the rest of them look like plumbers.

—Umpire Art Passarella

He's magic. To me, he's the most exciting player in the game. He does it too easy, in fact. He just wakes up, gets out of bed, comes out, and does it.

—All-Star Todd Helton on Rockies teammate Larry Walker, c. 1999, *Baseball Digest*

He puts the ball in play as good as anybody and has a knack for getting base hits. He always seems to be right there when the leaders are put on the board.

—Longtime manager and coach Bill Virdon on Todd Helton

Shouting on a ball field never helped anyone except when it was one player calling to another to take the catch.

—Dodgers star Gil Hodges, discounting the value of "chatter"

He never remembered a sign or forgot a newspaperman's name.

—Cubs manager Leo Durocher on Ernie Banks

I don't even see pitches down the middle anymore. Not even in batting practice.

—Hank Aaron as he approached Babe Ruth's career home run record

They can run like scalded cats. They spray the ball all over the field and are really tough to defend.

—Unidentified opposing manager on Lloyd and Paul Waner, Pirates hitting stars

It isn't hard to be good from time to time in sports. What's tough is being good every day.

—Giants great Willie Mays

When I first saw Roger [Clemens], it was spring training and I saw him warm up and thought, "Thank God that guy is on our team."

—Hall of Famer Wade Boggs on his Boston teammate from *The History of the Boston Red Sox* by Richard Rambeck

People from Sandusky [Ohio] don't drive here [Cleveland] to see Jim Thome bunt.

—Thome, quoting his Indians coach Grady Little on why he should never bunt versus the infield shift, from *Baseball Digest*, May 2003

Their only weakness is they can't hit balls rolled under the plate.

—Opposing manager Charlie Grimm on the Waners, Paul and Lloyd

I was a little nervous out there. It was like any opening day. I don't care how long you played—you always get a little nervous.

—Catching great Yogi Berra

[Ty] Cobb lived off the field as though he wished to live forever. He lived on the field as though it was his last day.

—Baseball executive Branch Rickey

My wife told me I've got 17 strikeouts in 23 at-bats against Pedro. I'm a major league hitter. I've faced the best pitchers in the game. I ought to be able to put the ball in play half the time.

—All-Star Travis Fryman

[Bob Feller] was the test. I'd sit in my room thinking and seeing him, thinking about him all that time. God, I loved it. That was a personal challenge.

—Superstar hitter Ted Williams, from *Summer of '49* by David Halberstam

We all come here with talent. But the stars are the ones who don't have to work at concentrating. The superstars are the ones who are unconscious. They're in a trance. That's what George was in.

—Royals designated hitter Hal McRae on George Brett's sizzling 1980 season

That [Willie] Davis is so fast his head's three feet behind the rest of him.

—Umpire Jocko Conlan

I'll take any way to get into the Hall of Fame. If they want a batboy, I'll go in as a batboy.

—Yankees infielder Phil Rizzuto

He's the only man I ever saw who was a cripple and could outdo the world.

—Yankee manager Casey Stengel on his superstar center fielder Mickey Mantle, from *The History of the New York Yankees* by Richard Rambeck

There are some great ballplayers, but there aren't any superstars. Superstars you find on the moon.

—Dodger coach Jim Gilliam

He says hello opening day, goodbye closing day and, in between, hits .350.

—Tiger great Mickey Cochrane on Charlie Gehringer

When you call a pitcher "Lefty" and everybody in both leagues knows who you mean, he must be pretty good.

—Royals outfielder Clint Hurdle on Phillies ace Steve Carlton

He could bunt .300 if he tried.

—Longtime manager Billy Martin on Rod Carew

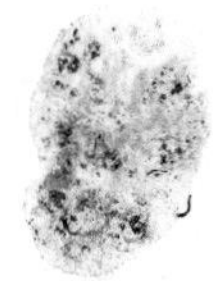

I once threw a side-arm [sic] spitter right into his belly and he hit it into the upper deck. I may have got Waner out, but I never fooled him.

—Burleigh Grimes on pitching to Paul Waner

Ty Cobb is a low-down, miserable excuse for a human being. He's also the greatest player I've ever seen.

—Tiger teammate Sam Crawford

Why ask me? Ask the kid if he'll pose with me!

—Star pitcher Dizzy Dean, when asked if he would pose for a picture with up-and-coming star Bob Feller, from *The History of the Cleveland Indians* by Richard Rambeck

He doesn't have many pitches, he's just got the one pitch, but he gets people out with that all the time. He's got such a nice, easy, relaxed motion, and when it comes out, it comes out on top of you.

—Pitcher Paul Shuey on Yankees closer Mariano Rivera

To him [Ty Cobb], a ballgame wasn't a mere athletic contest. It was a knock-'em-down, crush-'em, relentless war. He was their enemy and if they got in his way he ran right over them.

—Catcher Moe Berg

I don't think [Warren] Spahn will ever get into the Hall of Fame. He'll never stop pitching.

—Hall of Famer Stan Musial, 1965

Not many power pitchers still have the good fastball by the time they reach their mid-30s. But Roger is not your average guy. He's made of different stuff than you or I.

—Toronto pitcher Pat Hentgen on ace pitcher Roger Clemens, c. 1997

It would be presumptuous of me to describe what an artist does. It would be like asking an art student how Michelangelo paints.

—Manager Gene Mauch, when asked to discuss Carew's hitting

I've cheated, or someone on my team has cheated, in almost every game I've been in.

—Second baseman Rogers Hornsby

Rod Carew could get more hits with a soup bone than I could get with a rack full of bats. He can do anything he wants to up there.

—Minnesota teammate Steve Brye, from *The History of the Minnesota Twins* by Richard Rambeck

All I know is that if Sandy Koufax was pitching today, he wouldn't be able to count the money he'd be getting—he'd have to weigh it.

—Dodgers manager Tommy Lasorda

I don't want them to forget Ruth. I just want them to remember me.

—Hank Aaron, on becoming the all-time home run king

Spahn and Sain, then pray for rain.

—Widely quoted of Braves star pitchers Warren Spahn and Johnny Sain

I like to think of myself as a complete ballplayer. I'd like to be remembered as a good all-around player, not just as a fellow who hit home runs.

—Braves superstar Hank Aaron

Joe DiMaggio batting sometimes gave the impression—the suggestion— that the old rules and dimensions of baseball no longer applied to him and that the game had at last grown unfairly easy.

—Author Roger Angell, from his *The Summer Game*

When I saw my name on a Louisville Slugger bat, that was the greatest thrill I ever had.

—Red Sox superstar Ted Williams

Just throw the ball and duck.

—Manager John McGraw on how to pitch to Pirates shortstop Honus Wagner

[It's] a game within a game. I'm the mouse and the cats are trying to trap me.

—Maury Wills on stealing bases

He handled the bat with the same efficiency Merlin coaxed from his wand. Rod Carew was a baseball magician with the power to make well-placed pitches disappear into every conceivable outfield gap.

—From *Baseball's 100 Greatest Players*, *The Sporting News* publication

Hold on to your pants, or he'll steal those, too.

—Germany Schaefer on his teammate Ty Cobb

He is the kind of boy who makes his scout's job safe for years.

—Unidentified Dodger executive upon signing power hitter Gil Hodges

If I had one wish in the world today it would be that Jackie Robinson could be here to see this happen.

—Frank Robinson on becoming baseball's first African American manager

Barry Bonds's wrists, Vladimir Guerrero's arms, Cal Ripken's health, and Greg Maddux's brain.

—Outfielder Cliff Floyd on building the ideal ballplayer

From the standpoint of excitement and drawing power, Reggie and Pete Rose are in a class by themselves.

—Angels owner Gene Autry on Reggie Jackson

I have observed that baseball is not unlike war and when you get right down to it, we batters are the heavy artillery.

—Ty Cobb, twelve-time batting crown winner

You're trying your damndest, you strike out and they boo you. I act like it doesn't bother me, like I don't hear anything the fans say, but the truth is I hear every word of it and it kills me.

—Hall of Fame third baseman Mike Schmidt

Hershiser may never have another year like 1988. Maybe nobody ever will.

—Unidentified sportswriter on Cy Young Award–winner Orel Hershiser's record of 59 consecutive scoreless innings

That kid's too tough for me to catch. He throws that thing so fast it looks like a pea.

—Indians catcher Steve O'Neill on the seventeen-year-old Bob Feller

He talks okay up there with a bat in his hands. A college education don't do you no good up there [at the plate].

—Manager Casey Stengel on Yogi Berra

Nobody else would have played [with injuries like Mickey Mantle's]. Nobody. But Mickey isn't like normal people.

—Yankees catcher Elston Howard, from *The History of the New York Yankees* by Michael E. Goodman

Henry belongs in a higher league.

—Joe Torre on Braves teammate Hank Aaron

Somebody will have to come and tear the uniform off me and the guy who comes better have help.

—300-game winner Early Wynn on when he'd give up pitching

[Ty] Cobb stopped off on the way to the ballpark to have his spikes honed.

—Arthur Baer, baseball columnist

I watched him [Reggie Jackson] when I was ten and he hit three home runs in the World Series; he was flamboyant and he backed it up. And, actually, I can tolerate a lot of trash talking when somebody can back it up.

—Hitting coach Gerald Perry

I can remember a reporter asking for a quote and I didn't know what a quote was. I thought it was some kind of soft drink.

—Young Yankees star Joe DiMaggio

He's the only guy who puts fear into me. Not because he can get me out but because he could kill me.

—Slugger Reggie Jackson on Nolan Ryan

You wind him up on opening day and forget him.

—Unidentified Tiger teammate on Charlie "the Mechanical Man" Gehringer

You talk about a role model, this is a role model: Don't be like me. God gave me the ability to play baseball and I wasted it.

—Hall of Famer Mickey Mantle

He was the greatest shortstop I ever saw. He was afraid of nobody.

—Bob Feller on Indians star Lou Boudreau

He had about him a touch of royalty.

—Commissioner Bowie Kuhn on Pirates star Roberto Clemente

Your basic George Foster home run. It probably would have killed four people and broken three seats.

—Pirates catcher Ed Ott

When I began playing the game, baseball was about as gentlemanly as a kick in the crotch.

—Hall of Fame outfielder Ty Cobb

Every mistake I throw, [he] hits a home run. That doesn't seem fair. He can at least mix in a double every once in a while.

—Pitcher David Cone on Ken Griffey Jr.

[Dick] Allen is so strong he has arms like legs.

—Manager Gene Mauch

He's a pure baseball player. He knows nothing about stats. Reporters ask him about his numbers and when they leave, he'll say, "I don't know stats." He plays simply to win.

—Brewers manager Tom Trebelhorn on Robin Yount, from *The History of the Milwaukee Brewers* by Richard Rambeck

It's not fair for a guy to be that strong and yet so disciplined at the plate. I have no idea how to get him out.

—Detroit pitcher Jack Morris on Frank Thomas

I can't imagine Joe DiMaggio was a better all-around player than Dale Murphy.

—Nolan Ryan, strikeout king

You've got to remember, I'm seventy-three years old now.

—Ty Cobb in 1960, explaining why he had told a reporter if he was still playing he'd hit only .300, 67 points below his lifetime average

There's no meaning to this honor if you're not alive.

—Outfielder Earl Averill upon his induction into the Hall of Fame

Any time you think you have the game conquered, the game will turn around and punch you right in the nose.

—Hall of Fame third baseman Mike Schmidt

[Hank Aaron] was so consistent with his numbers. It was amazing the kind of performance he had; you don't see guys doing that any more—hitting .330, .340 every year and hitting 40 home runs. Now it happens one year and you're a superstar.

—Outfielder Roy White

He [Josh Gibson] could hit any pitch to any field. The only way to pitch to him was to throw the ball low and behind him.

—Negro Leagues pitcher Chet Brewer

They throw the ball, I hit it. They hit the ball, I catch it.

—Superstar Willie Mays

Lou Gehrig was the most valuable player the Yankees ever had because he was a prime source of their greatest asset: an implied confidence in themselves and in every man on the club. Lou's pride as a big leaguer rubbed off on every one who played with him.

—Sportswriter Stanley Frank

I'll say this, going from first to home, Jesse [Owens] wouldn't have beaten Cool Papa [Bell].

—Negro Leagues star Buck O'Neil

Somebody's gotta win and somebody's gotta lose—and I believe in letting the other guy lose.

—Batting champ Pete Rose

Fans don't boo nobodies.

—Outfielder Reggie Jackson

It wasn't a bad pitch, but it wasn't good enough against Hank Aaron.

—Cincinnati's Jack Billingham on giving up Aaron's record-tying 714th homer

CHAPTER FIVE

Fielding and Fielders

When it comes to the defensive side of the game, there are, as is the case with hitting and pitching, many fine quotes to be found. However, in this case, the quotations frequently tend to run to two extremes—there are the words of praise and hyperbole employed to describe the great gloves and then there are the words of humor and even derision to describe not the gold, but the iron gloves. It's a case of beauty and the butcher.

Therefore, this chapter, of course, includes kudos for the Ozzie Smiths, Johnny Benches, and Brooks Robinsons of baseball. After all, dazzling glovework elicits Fourth of July "ooohs" and "ahhhs" from the grandstand. So tribute must also be paid to Roberto Clemente, Willie Mays, et al.

On the other hand, this chapter is also peppered with comments about the men such as Babe Herman and Jose Canseco who share the ignominy of having fly balls ricochet off their heads—capers such as theirs evoke laugher and incredulity but should also be chronicled. For instance, in my book, *Baseball Oddities*, I wrote that on Canseco's strangest defensive close encounter with a baseball he "resembled a combination of a ballerina and a soccer player as he first pirouetted back on the ball before he 'headed' it. That is to say he actually had the ball bounce off his noggin and over the wall for perhaps the most bizarre home run ever." That misadventure prompted Cleveland's general manager John Hart to mutter, "In my life I've never seen anything like that. I was stunned. I've seen balls hit outfielders on the head before, but not one that bounced over the fence." And, when reporters asked Texas infielder Julio Franco if he had ever seen such an odd play, he simply said, "Yeah, in a cartoon."

So, thanks to blooper films, fans can delight in zany misplays, perhaps taking solace that even big leaguers can botch a play or two. "Why, I coulda caught *that* ball," a fan might boast, no doubt deluding himself. Further, thanks to the vast media coverage of the game nowadays and special features such as Web Gems,

fans can also marvel at the athleticism of contemporary glove magicians.

Therefore, from gloves that go "clank" to the gloves of gold, here's the opportunity to take a look and a figurative listen to quotations involving fielders and the act of fielding.

Two-thirds of the earth is covered by water. The other one-third is covered by Garry Maddox.

—Ralph Kiner, announcer, on outfielder Garry Maddox

I bet he couldn't make that play again, not even on instant replay.

—Second sacker Red Schoendienst of outfielder Roberto Clemente, also attributed to others (e.g., Bill Virdon on Lou Brock)

A good catcher is the quarterback, the carburetor, the lead dog, the pulse taker, the traffic cop, and sometimes a lot of unprintable things, but no team gets very far without one.

—Manager Miller Huggins

His arms are too short. He makes easy plays look hard.

—Joe McCarthy, Yankees manager, on his first baseman Babe Dahlgren

When I throw a ground ball, I expect it to be an out—maybe two.

—Pitcher Warren Spahn

I hear it [the car Brooks Robinson won as the 1970 World Series MVP] has an oversized glove compartment.

—Reds catcher Johnny Bench

My teammates have nicknamed me "Retriever." All I ever seem to be doing is going back to the screen.

—Atlanta catcher Bruce Benedict on chasing down knuckleballs

My best pitch is anything the batter grounds, lines, or pops in the direction of Phil Rizzuto.

—Yankees pitcher Vic Raschi on his teammate

The infield is like a steel net held in the hands of the catcher. He is the psychologist and historian for the staff.

—Writer Jacques Barzun in "God's Country and Mine," from *The Baseball Reader* by Charles Einstein

What I've seen over the past fifteen to twenty years is that the quickest route to the major leagues is by being a catcher.

—Veteran catcher Ray Hayworth

I had some advice for another fielder and I shouted it at the top of my lungs. . . . "Catch it. Catch it or I'll kill you."

—Hall of Fame outfielder Willie Mays on a routine fly to the outfield to end the regular season and thrust his Giants into the 1951 playoffs, from *Willie Mays: My Life in and Out of Baseball* by Charles Einstein

The next time he [a man posing as Babe Herman] comes in, take him out in the backyard and knock a few flies his way. If he catches any, you'll know it isn't me.

—Outfielder Babe Herman, making fun of his defensive ineptitude to a bank teller

One year I led the National League in errors. They named a vitamin after me that year—One-a-Day.

—Cubs infielder Roy Smalley

He [Roberto Clemente] had that great arm, but I really don't understand how it held up, because when we'd take infield he'd throw like the game depended on it.

—Pirates outfielder Bill Virdon, from *Tales from the Ballpark* by Mike Shannon

The minute his glove touches the ball, it's out of his hands and on the way either to the infield or the plate. I've never seen a man get the ball back into play so fast.

—Cubs manager Stan Hack on Willie Mays

I've seen a lot of third basemen, and don't get me wrong, I don't get carried away, but you could make a highlight tape of the plays he's made this year [2006] and it would be second to nobody's.

—Tiger manager Jim Leyland on Brandon Inge, from *USA Today Sports Weekly*

Jorge Orta never got acquainted with his glove, never met a ground ball he liked.

—White Sox executive Paul Richards

His [Thurman Munson's] greatest asset is not his bat. It is his incredible ability to get rid of the ball. It sometimes seems that he throws it before he has caught it.

—From a story in *Newsday*

I can't play perfect every day.

—Infielder Teddy Martinez after committing five errors over five contests

The key step for an infielder is the first one—to the left or right, but before the ball is hit.

—Manager Earl Weaver

I fought the wall and the wall won.

—Outfielder Dmitri Young after crashing into the wall in pursuit of a fly ball

It was his solemn duty to catch a ball that wasn't in the stands.

—Outfielder Monte Irvin on his Giants teammate Willie Mays

What was I supposed to say? Glad you got over Watergate?

—Second baseman Steve Sax, regarding former President Nixon's having commented he was glad Sax overcame his throwing difficulties

The catcher is the physical and emotional focus of every baseball game; he faces outward, surveying and guiding it all and everyone else on the team looks in at him.

—Author Roger Angell, from *Late Innings*

You see that cement in front of your house? Paint it green and jump on it. That's how it feels.

—Outfielder Lenny Dykstra on how making a diving catch on Astroturf feels

Defense is baseball's visible poetry and its invisible virtue.

—Writer Thomas Boswell

I can't very well tell my batters, "Don't hit it to him." Wherever they hit it, he's there anyway.

—Manager Gil Hodges on center fielder Willie Mays

He fields better on one leg than anybody else I got on two.

—Mets manager Casey Stengel of his first baseman Gil Hodges

I don't feel it is too hard. Shortstop is hard. When you play shortstop, you can play everywhere.

—Tigers shortstop Carlos Guillen on filling in for the regular first baseman Sean Casey in 2006

There isn't anything to the pivot [on a double play], if you have guts enough to stand there.

—Infielder Rod Kanehl, from *The Jocks* by Leonard Shecter

He's the guts of the Angels, our triple threat: he can hit, run, and lob.

—Merv Rettenmund as a coach, on Don Baylor

Statistics say he was the second best second baseman in the league, but that doesn't count the balls he couldn't get to.

—Manager Dick Williams on Juan Bonilla

If a woman has to choose between catching a fly ball and saving an infant's life, she will choose to save the infant's life without even considering if there are men on base.

—Humorist Dave Barry

I was out there mowing the lawn during the [players'] strike. I got the front yard done and half the backyard and I kept waiting for Sam Mejias to come out and finish it for me.

—Reds outfielder Dave Collins, accustomed to being yanked for defensive purposes late in games

The secret of my success was clean living and a fast-moving outfield.

—Lefty Gomez, Hall of Fame pitcher

Don't hit it to me.

—Outfielder Jose Canseco when asked how his team could improve defensively

Clomping around in the outfield, he [Frank Howard] catches hell from crowds more than he catches anything else.

—Writer Ron Smith

There are some fielders who make the impossible catch look ordinary and some the ordinary catch look impossible.

—Manager Joe McCarthy

I'd like to see him do it again.

—Manager Charlie Dressen after Willie Mays robbed his team of extra bases on a sensational catch

His [Johnny Bench's] shortstop-quick hands and his smoothness and balance and mobility behind the plate instantly caused all the catchers in the land to imitate his one-handed style, but none of them, then or now, could touch him.

—Writer Roger Angell

Do not alibi on bad hops; anybody can field the good ones.

—Pitcher Chief Bender, but also attributed to manager Joe McCarthy

I'd rather have a Gold Glove than a Silver Slugger. Defense is so much more of a team game.

—Infielder Alex Rodriguez, from *www.baseballalmanac.com*

Luis Aparicio is the only guy that I ever saw go behind second base, make the turn, and throw Mickey Mantle out. He was as sure-handed as anyone.

—Yankees infielder Phil Rizzuto

I was a pudgy kid. That [catcher's position] was the only place for me to play.

—All-time great Josh Gibson

I tried to jump as high as I can, but I knew I had like a 10 percent chance in my mind that I could catch it. I improvised and did it on the run. See the ball. See the wall. Do the thing that I've got to do.

—Mets outfielder Endy Chavez on his great leaping catch in Game Seven of the 2006 NLCS

When you have hands as bad as mine, one hand is better than two.

—Outfielder Ken Harrelson on his one-handed catches

My wife got tired of sharing me with another woman.

—Mel Hall, outfielder, on why he no longer used his glove, which he named Lucille

Pop flies, in a sense, are just a diversion for a second baseman. Grounders are his stock in trade.

—Infielder Jackie Robinson

So-so in center field.

—Article in the *Daily News* about Willie Mays after he appeared in his first big-league game

When a fielder gets a pitcher in trouble, the pitcher has to pitch himself out of a slump he isn't in.

—Manager Casey Stengel

A catcher and his body are like the outlaw and his horse. He's got to ride that nag till it drops.

—Hall of Fame catcher Johnny Bench

If you prefer baseball in slow motion, don't miss George Foster chasing a double into the left-field corner.

—Sportswriter Charles Bricker

Catching a fly ball is a pleasure, but knowing what to do with it after you catch it is a business.

—Yankees outfielder Tommy Henrich

A guy that makes errors is a guy who gets to a lot of balls that other guys can't get to and most of the time his errors aren't going to be caused by trying to make the play, it'll be trying to make the throw and it got away.

—Jesse Orosco, ace reliever

I don't want to embarrass any other catcher by comparing him with Johnny Bench.

—Sparky Anderson, manager of the Reds

We took his glove to the chapel this morning. We got the devil out of it.

—Outfielder Terry Puhl on Houston teammate Enos Cabell

The sun was a problem, but not even sunglasses would have helped Albert [Belle] on that play. He would have needed an eclipse.

—Cleveland manager Mike Hargrove on his outfielder losing a fly ball, from *Indians on the Game* by Wayne Stewart

I look up in the stands and I see them [fans] miss balls, too.

—Outfielder Devon White on being booed for a misplay

The man with the ball is responsible for what happens to the ball.

—Baseball executive Branch Rickey on his belief that the pitcher should have the final say on what pitch to throw

If you hit [Luis] Polonia a hundred fly balls, you could make a movie out of it—*Catch-22*.

—Pitcher Dennis Lamp

It wastes time to straighten up.

—William "Buck" Ewing, said to be the first catcher to make his throws to second while in his crouch, from *Baseball's Hall of Fame* by Robert Smith

There's nothing tough about playing third. All a guy needs is a strong arm and a strong chest.

—Pirates manager Frankie Frisch

He wasn't supposed to hit it over there.

—Yankees outfielder Roberto Kelly on his inability to track down a double

It's not that Reggie [Jackson] is a bad outfielder. He just has trouble judging the ball and picking it up.

—Billy Martin, once Jackson's manager

Let's put it this way—pigeons have been roosting on him for two years.

—Broadcaster Vin Scully on Ron Cey's defense at third base

Why should I go jack-knifing over the fence on my head? That ball has got no business being out there 400 feet.

—Outfielder Reggie Smith

I didn't start catching until I was a senior in high school . . . I was the only guy dumb enough to go behind the plate.

—Duke Sims, Cleveland catcher, from *the Sporting News*, August 22, 1970

I don't compare them, I just catch them.

—Center fielder Willie Mays, when asked how his 1954 World Series classic catch ranked among his best ever

[Jim] Thome said I looked pretty good and Richie [Sexson] said I looked like crap. Richie's a little more blunt.

—Cleveland third baseman Travis Fryman of his debut playing first base, from *the Chronicle-Telegram* of June 12, 2000

A great catch is like watching girls go by. The last one you see is always the prettiest.

—Pitcher Bob Gibson

The fans may be surprised to know that during my freshman year at Oglethorpe, I waited on tables and never made an error, never dropped a tray nor broke a dish.

—Shortstop Luke Appling

He plays the outfield like he's trying to catch grenades.

—Reggie Jackson on fellow outfielder Claudell Washington

For eight of his first nine seasons he led the American League in fielding and rarely fell below one hundred double plays a year. Not endowed with great speed, Lou made up for it with his quick start and more than that with his extraordinary ability to read the hitters.

—On Cleveland shortstop Lou Boudreau, from *Mitts* by William Curran

When one of his tosses almost killed a peanut vendor in the twenty-sixth row, the coaches handed him an outfielder's glove.

—Pitcher Bill Lee on infielder Juan Beniquez

Good defense in baseball is like good umpiring: It's there, you expect it, but you don't really appreciate it. But when it isn't there, then you notice it.

—Infielder Doug DeCinces

Willie Mays's glove is where triples go to die.

—Sportswriter Jim Murray, also attributed to announcer Vin Scully, and to Fresco Thompson as "Willie Mays and his glove: where triples go to die."

He plays second base like Ozzie Smith played short.

—Pitcher David Wells on Robbie Alomar, from *Baseball Digest*, June 1996

If I did anything funny on the ball field, it was strictly accidental. Like the way I played third base. Some people thought it was hilarious, but I was on the level all the time.

—Longtime player and minor league manager Rocky Bridges

The only way I'm going to get a Gold Glove is with a can of spray paint.

—Reggie Jackson

We always used to make sure to mention in our pre-game meeting that he was the one guy you don't test out there.

—Ace pitcher Kevin Brown on rifle-armed outfielder Raul Mondesi, from *Baseball Digest*, September 1999

The way to get a hit past Honus [Wagner] is to hit it eight feet over his head.

—Manager John McGraw

I don't care how big they make the gloves, you still have to catch the ball.

—Ethan Allen, outfielder

I look at it this way—suppose those thirty pitches had been balls? Then I would have had no errors [in 1979].

—Third baseman George Brett

In the outfield, fly balls are my only weakness.

—Journeyman Carmelo Martinez, also listed as "The only problem I have in the outfield is with fly balls."

They didn't give him a cake. They were afraid he'd drop it.

—Casey Stengel, Mets manager, concerning the Mets team birthday party for Marv Throneberry

He can play all three outfield positions—at the same time.

—Manager Gene Mauch of Houston's Cesar Cedeno

His only limitation is his ability to move around.

—St. Louis manager Joe Torre on outfielder Pedro Guerrero

He reacted to the ball with the speed of a sedated hippo.

—Sportswriter Lowel Cohn on Giants outfielder Jack Clark

Errors are a part of the game, but Abner Doubleday was a jerk for inventing them.

—Journeyman Billy Ripken

Every play he made was executed so gracefully that it looked like it was the easiest thing in the world.

—Unidentified Detroit Tiger on Nap Lajoie

Errors are a part of my image. One night in Pittsburgh, thirty-thousand fans gave me a standing ovation when I caught a hotdog wrapper on the fly.

—Poor defensive first baseman Dick Stuart

Those guys are incredible. There's never been a twosome like them before and for my money, I don't think you'll see anybody as good ever again.

—Tiger manager Sparky Anderson on his double play combo of Lou Whitaker and Alan Trammell

Never once did I get hit on the head by a fly ball. Once or twice on the shoulder maybe, but never on the head.

—Babe Herman, defending his terrible defense

He hasn't got much range, but what he can get to, he'll drop.

—Unidentified teammate of Harmon Killebrew

What are you trying to do, take my fans away from me?

—Terrible defender Marv Throneberry of the Mets to teammate Frank Thomas, who had just made two errors on a play

You have to analyze a hitter a bit more carefully than before. You have to know exactly where to play him because your range is drastically reduced [on artificial turf]. Only the smartest infielders will survive on the stuff.

—Shortstop Bud Harrelson

Bobby Brown reminds me of a fellow who's been hitting for twelve years and fielding one.

—Yankees manager Casey Stengel

What do the Giants and Michael Jackson have in common? Answer—they both wear a glove for no apparent reason.

—Popular joke, c. 1990.

In one of the first throwing contests on record during a benefit game at Fenway Park, Jackson out threw all the prominent outfielders of his time, including Ruth, Speaker and Cobb.

—Author William Curran, from his book *Mitts* on "Shoeless Joe" Jackson

First, I pray to God that nobody hits the ball to me. Then, I pray to God nobody hits the ball to Steve Sax.

—Shaky third baseman Pedro Guerrero, when asked what he is thinking about in a late, tight situation while his Dodgers are in the field

It's like playing in front of a mirror. Everything seems backwards.

—Outfielder Larry Walker on playing left field as opposed to playing right field, from *Indians on the Game* by Wayne Stewart

The A's need a hit or a Boston mistake. If they are looking for a Boston mistake, I suggest they don't hit it to [Jerry] Remy.

—Announcer Lon Simmons

When one of them guys hits a single to you, throw the ball to third. That way we can hold them to a double.

—Manager Casey Stengel on his inept outfielders during his Mets inaugural season of 1962

It was as if his hands never touched the ball. As soon as the ball reached his glove it was on its way to first base. Frankly, I never saw anything like it.

—Bill Mazeroski's Pirates double play partner, Dick Groat

I think it is generally true that all power-hitting shortstops get a bad rap as defensive players. In our own time, Cal Ripken, Roy Smalley and Robin Yount have all been, in my opinion, far better defensive shortstops than they got credit for being.

—Baseball analyst Bill James, from his book *The Bill James Historical Baseball Abstract*

You don't get a hell of a lot of practice. It's not easy to find guys who'll come out early before games and run into you.

—Catcher Mike Scioscia, an outstanding plate blocker, on how he got so good at that facet of defense

Get in front of those balls; you won't get hurt. That's what you've got a chest for, young man.

—Giants manager John McGraw

It's like if you go to another country and they drive on the left side of the road. I can do it, but I might make a couple of mistakes.

—David Justice, outfielder, on switching from right field to left field, from the *Chronicle-Telegram*, June 11, 2000

The first thing you want in a catcher is ability to handle the pitchers. Then you want defensive skill and, of course, the good arm. Last of all, if he can hit with power, well, then you've got a Johnny Bench.

—Orioles general manager Frank Cashen

Artificial turf has taken away the great plays but also the bad hops. You used to see good fielders able to adjust, but on turf, everything is more mechanical. Turf makes good fielders into great ones and turns poor fielders into good fielders . . .

—Star shortstop Mark Belanger

Every time [Johnny] Bench throws, everybody in baseball drools.

—Baltimore Orioles general manager Harry Dalton

He [Bobby Brown] had such lousy hands when he played third, I wouldn't want him to operate on me.

—Infielder Gene Woodling, teammate of Brown who, in fact, was an MD

He [Graig Nettles] makes unbelievable plays, half in defense of his life, half just in defense.

—Yankees pitcher Sparky Lyle

We got a guy on our club who has such bad hands his glove is embarrassed.

—Phillies pitcher Frank Sullivan

If I won a Gold Glove, that thing might sit in front of my house bronzed.

—Pirates poor defensive third baseman Bobby Bonilla

CHAPTER SIX

Managers and Managing

It's a very exclusive club, the circle of men who run big-league teams. After all, at any given time there are only thirty human beings on the face of the planet who hold the occupation of big league manager—and their hold on that title is often quite tenuous. Their job description and duties run the gamut from the handling of men (many of them temperamental with colossal egos), to dealing with a global and ever more demanding media, to actually doing what managers almost universally say they love doing the most and which they actually find to be the easiest part of their job: the running of the team on the field, the guiding their players through games, constantly making split-second decisions, and playing that baseball/chess game of planning several innings ahead.

The men who have held down this job have come from diverse backgrounds. Bob Boone, for instance, holds a degree in psychology yet contends that hasn't really helped him as a manager. "I don't think there's a direct correlation . . . it's not like, 'Gee, you went to Stanford and you have a degree in psychology, therefore you're an expert and you can psychoanalyze everybody.' I think that's completely a farce . . ."

Meanwhile, many managers of the early days of baseball were far from being well educated, some never even finished high school. Casey Stengel may have been called the Old Professor, but listening to him for just a few seconds would reveal he was hardly a scholar.

Of course, men such as Stengel were, in a baseball sense, quite cerebral (see Warren Spahn's more fitting take on Stengel in this chapter). Luckily, too, many managers possess a wonderful sense of humor (necessary when combating the tribulations of their job), sometimes sharp and sarcastic, other times self-deprecating and, best of all, often just downright hilarious.

So, it's time to delve into the world of minor and major league managers and to take in the humor as well as the insights their words reveal.

If I were playing third base and my mother were rounding third with the run that was going to beat us, I'd trip her. Oh, I'd pick her up and brush her off and say, "Sorry, Mom," but nobody beats me.

—Fiery manager Leo Durocher

This ain't football. We do this every day.

—Manager Earl Weaver

There'll be two buses leaving the hotel for the park tomorrow. The 2:00 bus will be for those of you who need a little extra work. The empty bus will leave at 5:00.

—Giants manager Dave Bristol

The last baseball manager to make an original move was Zack Taylor in 1951. He sent a midget to bat for the St. Louis Browns.

—Authors Dan Daly and Bob O'Donnell, from *The Pro Football Chronicle*

Hold them for a few innings, fellas. I'll think of something.

—Confident manager Charlie Dressen, also attributed to John McGraw

It's games like this that make you want to see a ten-run rule enforced.

—Cardinals manager Whitey Herzog

Aren't all managers interim?

—Orioles pitcher Mike Flanagan

The rules are made by me, but I don't have to follow them.

—Manager Billy Martin

I'm on record saying this guy is the best I've ever been around. I told him, "I don't know anybody I've ever met in baseball in forty years who could take a club from where they were into the playoff and then beat the Yankees." He's got the gift, man.

—Cardinals manager Tony La Russa on Tigers manager Jim Leyland in 2006, when Detroit won 95 games, just three years after dropping 119 games, from the *Detroit Free Press*

I don't think, in all the years I managed them, I ever spoke more than thirty words to Frank and Brooks Robinson.

—Baltimore manager Earl Weaver

Gene Mauch's stare can put you on the disabled list.

—Catcher Tim McCarver

You only win with talent.

—Manager Sparky Anderson

There are only two things a manager needs to know: when to change pitchers and how to get along with your players.

—Senators manager Bucky Harris

When I first came up as a manager I was too damn demanding. I had to learn never to expect a man to do something he is not capable of doing. Now I try to analyze and find out their capabilities and then never ask to exceed them.

—Pirates manager Danny Murtaugh, winner of the 1960 Series

He [Ty Cobb] was so great himself that he couldn't understand why if he told players how to do certain things, they couldn't do it as well as he did.

—Hall of Famer Charlie Gehringer

We could finish first or in an asylum.

—Frankie Frisch, manager of the Gashouse Gang Cardinals of the 1930s.

One place I won't allow my players to drink is at the hotel where we're staying. That's where I do my drinking.

—Manager Casey Stengel, also attributed to A's manager Hank Bauer

When Leo [Durocher] touched his nose, it meant the hit-and-run was on. But there was one problem—the son of a gun was always picking his nose.

—Herman Franks, former catcher

I used to send myself up to pinch-hit whenever the wind was blowing out from home plate.

—Player-manager Joe Cronin

I reckon I tried everything on the old apple [baseball] but salt and pepper and chocolate sauce topping.

—Pitcher Gaylord Perry

You gotta lose 'em sometime. When you do, lose 'em right.

—Manager Casey Stengel

The greatest feeling in the world is to win a major league game. The second-greatest feeling is to lose a major league game.

—Manager Chuck Tanner

Victory may not be worth the price, if the price is Billy Martin.

—Thomas Boswell, from his *Game Day*

Give me my kind of team and we'll win.

—Manager Leo Durocher to Giants owner Horace Stoneham in 1948, from *The Image of Their Greatness* by Lawrence Ritter and Donald Honig

He [Cap Anson] was one of the first to use coaching signals, the hit-and-run, a pitching rotation and spring training. He was also a mean-spirited guy who . . . demanded very strict behavior.

—Unidentified sportswriter, from *The History of the Chicago Cubs* by Aaron Frisch

Even though I have loyalty to people, you have to be loyal to twenty-five players as opposed to just one.

—Yankees manager Joe Torre

You couldn't fool Casey [Stengel] because he'd pulled every stunt that ever was thought up and he did it fifty years before we even got there.

—Yankees great Mickey Mantle

The only thing that kept Jack Perconte from being a good major league player is performance.

—Manager Del Crandall

You're asking the wrong guy. I was in a lifelong slump.

—Manager Jim Leyland when asked about his team's hitting slump in Pittsburgh

[Paul] Molitor didn't walk across the lake to get here and he didn't change his clothes in the phone booth. He's just another tough hitter.

—Manager Doc Edwards to his Indians

We need three kinds of pitching: left-handed, right-handed, and relief.

—St. Louis manager Whitey Herzog, 1980

If you do the screaming, the players won't. If you get thrown out, they won't. You've got to keep the players in the lineup.

—Earl Weaver, Orioles manager

I think we can win it—if my brains hold out.

—Giants manager John McGraw in the thick of a pennant race

There goes Rick Monday. He and Manny Mota are so old that they were waiters at the Last Supper.

—Dodgers skipper Tommy Lasorda

If I were captain of the Titanic, I would tell my passengers we were stopping for ice.

—Pirates manager Chuck Tanner

I cussed him out in Spanish and he threw me out in English.

—Manager Lou Piniella on umpire Armando Rodriguez

I'm not one of those old-timers who say everything was better in my day. I think ballplayers today are better than the players were when I played. But what ever happened to "sit down, shut up, and listen"?

—Leo Durocher, longtime big-league manager

I don't understand how anyone hits a baseball. You play golf and the damn thing is sitting there and all you've got to do is hit it and that's hard enough.

—Coach and manager Ray Miller

You never unpack your suitcase in this business.

—Manager Preston Gomez upon being fired

You clowns could go on *What's My Line* in full uniforms and stump the panel.

—Pirates manager Billy Meyer of his pathetic crew

I think there should be bad blood between all clubs.

—Orioles manager Earl Weaver

Our D.L. [disabled list] was full before the first week [of the season] was done. I knew we were in trouble when the only sign we got was for the "hit and limp" play.

—Manager Clint Hurdle on a team he once was on

If he [Tony La Russa] doesn't win over there [with Oakland], he should be sued for malpractice.

—Pitcher Tommy John

He [Jerry Lumpe] looks like the greatest hitter in the world till you play him.

—Manager Casey Stengel

One of the main things that helped me later on as a manager is that as a player I was a catcher. . . . I think catchers should make good managers because they are the ones who direct the whole game. Everything is right there in front of them.

—Manager Al Lopez, from *Baseball Digest*, February 1988

In the 13 years I managed in the big leagues, they [umpires] must have made a million calls—and they were wrong just ninety-one times.

—Earl Weaver, Orioles manager, alluding to the 91 times he was kicked out of games

Casey Stengel had more baseball brains in his little finger than any other manager I knew had in their whole body.

—Outfielder Tommy Holmes

When fans come to the ballpark, damn it, every last one of them is a manager.

—Whitey Herzog, long-time skipper

Managing is not running, hitting, stealing. Managing is getting your players to put out 100 percent year after year.

—Reds manager Sparky Anderson

It's better to lose a game by making a move than lose it sitting on my ass.

—Orioles manager Earl Weaver, from his book *Winning!*

We need just two players to be a contender—Babe Ruth and Sandy Koufax.

—Manager Whitey Herzog, then with the Rangers

I don't give a hoot whether a guy likes me or not. I don't care what he does off the field or what kind of problems he creates for other people. If he comes to play, that's all I ask.

—Manager Leo Durocher, from *The Baseball Almanac* by Dan Schlossberg

I don't throw the first punch. I throw the second four.

—A's manager Billy Martin

Son, I think maybe we've had our workout for the day, don't you?

—Senators manager Bucky Harris, ready to lift his pitcher, who had issued walks to the game's first seven hitters

I thought I had the cure for cancer or something.

—Joe Torre, Yankees manager, several days after his team lost the 2006 American League Division Series to Detroit, when a slew of camera crews lined up outside his home, anticipating his being fired

I feel greatly honored to have a ballpark named after me, especially since I've been thrown out of so many.

—Manager Casey Stengel

Do you know what the average tenure is among big league managers? Two and a half years. Migrant fruit picking is more secure than that.

—From *Catcher in the Wry* by Bob Uecker

My boy, one small breeze doesn't make a windstorm.

—New York Giants manager John McGraw to a rookie

I'm forty-nine and I want to live to be fifty.

—Phillies manager Eddie Sawyer on his retirement (on an opening day after a defeat)

I managed good, but, boy, did they play bad.

—Minor league manager Rocky Bridges

Managing isn't all that difficult. Just score more runs than the other guy.

—Braves owner Ted Turner, who managed his club for one game and lost

The depth of his frown is in direct proportion to the length of his losing streak.

—Pitcher Jim Brosnan of Reds manager Fred Hutchinson

With a superstar, as long as you come play hard for Lou [Piniella] and show up at the ballpark and you perform everyday, he's not going to have a problem with you.

—Mariners first baseman Tino Martinez

I've got nothing against the bunt—in its place. But most of the time, that place is at the bottom of a long-forgotten closet.

—Orioles manager Earl Weaver

You don't worry about injuries this time of year. We're in a pennant race. If you can walk, you can play.

—Mets manager Davey Johnson

When I get through managing, I'm going to open up a kindergarten.
—Manager Billy Martin

Joe [Torre] lets players play and coaches coach.
—Yankees coach Don Zimmer

[Discipline is] the biggest secret to being a successful manager. You have to respect the players and the players have to respect you.
—Hall of Famer Al Lopez, from *Baseball Digest*, February 1988

All managers are losers—they are the most expendable pieces of furniture on earth.
—Hall of Famer Ted Williams

The way we're going, we had to do something.
—Bill Veeck on Lou Boudreau's explanation for playing hunches, from *Veeck as in Wreck* by Veeck with Ed Linn

Losing streaks are funny. If you lose at the beginning, you get off to a bad start. If you lose in the middle of the season, you're in a slump. If you lose at the end, you're choking.

—Manager Gene Mauch, whose 1964 Phillies folded down the stretch

Dick [Williams] told us at the beginning that team play was in and excuses were out. If you produced, you played. Simple as that.

—Padres catcher Terry Kennedy on his manager's philosophy, from *The History of the San Diego Padres* by Michael E. Goodman

You argue with an umpire because there's nothing else you can do about it.

—Manager Leo Durocher

Managers are hired to be fired.

—Angels manager Lefty Phillips

I really like this TV [color commentator] gig because asking the questions is a lot more fun than having to answer them.

—Lou Piniella, working 2006 playoffs, from *USA Today*

I'm not going to give them a Knute Rockne, let's go get 'em type of thing. I can tell you that right now.

—Detroit manager Jim Leyland, entering the final series of the 2006 season, battling for a division title

Say you were standing with one foot in the oven and one foot in an ice bucket. According to percentage people, you should be perfectly comfortable.

—Manager Bobby Bragan

Managing is getting paid for home runs someone else hits.

—Hall of Famer Casey Stengel

Baseball is like driving. It's the one who gets home safely that counts.

—Dodgers manager Tommy Lasorda

If we can discipline ourselves to do the little things right, the big things will take care of themselves.

—Giants manager Roger Craig, from *The History of the San Francisco Giants* by Aaron Frisch

My wife doesn't have to buy shoes at a garage sale anymore.

—Manager Doc Edwards of the difference between the salaries of a coach and a manager

I've always said I could manage Adolf Hitler, Benito Mussolini, and Hirohito. That doesn't mean I'd like them, but I'd manage them.

—Yankees skipper Billy Martin

Ticket sales will go up by at least two—my mom and dad.

—Fredi Gonzalez after being named the new skipper for the Marlins for the 2007 season

If you ain't got a bullpen, you ain't got nothin'.

—Manager Yogi Berra

I don't want guys who just try hard. I tried hard and I didn't get out of A-ball.

—Manager Jim Leyland

Sometimes I think I'm in the greatest business in the world. Then you lose four straight and want to change places with the farmer.

—Yankees manager Joe McCarthy

Most pitchers are too smart to manage.

—Ace pitcher Jim Palmer

Baseball has got to be fun, because if it's not fun, it's a long time to be in agony.

—Manager Tom Trebelhorn, from *Men at Work* by George F. Will

I treat all my players alike. I can't have two sets of rules.

—Rogers Hornsby as the St. Louis Browns manager

Another club can be beating you for six innings but for some reason the good ballclubs get tough and win them in the last three.

—Texas manager Billy Martin

There are only two kinds of managers. Winning managers and ex-managers.

—Gil Hodges, Mets manager

Between owners and players, a manager today has become a wishbone.

—Pitcher John Curtis, from *Sports Illustrated*

It's like a child doing something bad at the dinner table. You send him to bed without dinner, but he's back down for breakfast in the morning.

—Yankees owner George Steinbrenner on rehiring Gene Michael

That midget can barely see over the top of the dugout steps and he claims he can see the pitches. He blames every loss on the players, the umpires, or the ground conditions.

—Umpire Marty Springstead on Earl Weaver

If you are so smart, how come you are still in the Army?

—Manager Casey Stengel to a soldier who had complained about Stengel's strategies

Bill [McKechnie] taught me the secret of [managerial] success is earning the respect of your men. Respect and good pitching.

—Manager Al Lopez, from *The Baseball Almanac* by Dan Schlossberg

If we had been traveling by train, I probably would have done that [held his manager off a moving train] to [Earl] Weaver. Unfortunately, you don't want to do it out of an airplane.

—Orioles pitching ace Jim Palmer of the supposed story of Babe Ruth holding Miller Huggins off a train

If he made me a consultant five minutes ago, my first recommendation would have been not to fire the manager.

—John Wathan after being fired as the Royals manager and then being offered a job as a consultant to the team

Son, it ain't the water cooler that's striking you out.

—Yankees skipper Casey Stengel to a young Mickey Mantle, who was taking out his anger on inanimate objects

A manager really gets paid for how much he suffers.

—Cleveland executive Gabe Paul

I'm not buddy-buddy with the players. If they need a buddy, let them buy a dog.

—Manager Whitey Herzog

You know when you got it made? When you get your name in the crossword puzzle.

—Minor league manager Rocky Bridges

Ask anyone in this clubhouse who they'd bleed for and it would be Bobby Cox.

—Atlanta's Todd Pratt

They've taken my playing record off and put my managerial record on.

—Sparky Anderson, manager, on why he liked the latest set of baseball cards

I've never been wrong yet. They just didn't execute what I wanted them to do.
—Manager Chuck Tanner

I don't give a damn about the color of a man's skin. I'm only interested in how well or how badly he plays this game.
—Manager Leo Durocher

All of you guys, when you get into the locker room I want you to check your locker. He [Jackie Robinson] stole everything out there he wanted to today so he might have stole your jockstraps as well.
—Manager Casey Stengel

He was more of a movie star. I think you can get caught up in that [Hollywood] stuff and not worry so much about winning.
—Pitcher Dennis Cook on Tommy Lasorda

The safety squeeze is a tough play—you're willing to take gambles, take risks, but to me the safety squeeze is one of those where you better be really desperate if you're going to use it.

—Cleveland manager Mike Hargrove

Being with a woman all night never hurt no professional baseball player. It's the staying up all night looking for one that does him in.

—Manager Casey Stengel

Don't find many faults with the umpire. You can't expect him to be as perfect as you are.

—Yankees manager Joe McCarthy

Lou [Piniella] has three rules for us—to be on time, play heads up and, uh, I forgot the third.

—Infielder Todd Benzinger of his manager with the Reds

I don't fine players. These days if I fine a 4 million dollar player four hundred dollars, he's liable to tip me $200.

—Florida manager Jim Leyland

If a manager of mine ever said someone was indispensable, I'd fire him.

—Oakland owner Charlie Finley

Yeah, and we're missing a little geography and arithmetic around here, too.

—St. Louis manager Whitey Herzog on his team's poor chemistry

Let me do the worrying.

—Yankees manager Joe McCarthy

Leo Durocher is a man with an infinite capacity for immediately making a bad thing worse.

—Baseball executive Branch Rickey, also seen as "He can take a bad situation and make it immediately worse."

This is the first time I was ever outmanaged on an offday.

—Tigers manager Jim Leyland of Yankee skipper Joe Torre after an American League Divison Series game between the two clubs was called off—Torre sent his players home but Leyland, not yet aware of the cancellation, had his pitchers long-tossing, preparing for the game

I got one [catcher] that can throw but can't catch and one that can catch but can't throw and one who can hit but can't do either.

—Mets skipper Casey Stengel

It's a lousy job. No matter who you pick, you're going to be condemned.

—Billy Martin on managing the All-Star Game

Tell a ballplayer something a thousand times. Then tell him again because that might be the time he'll understand something.

—Manager Paul Richards

If a man knows he's played bad ball and won't admit it, he shouldn't be out there.

—Giants manager Leo Durocher

I could never be a manager. I can't manage myself. What would I do with twenty-five other problems?

—Yankees superstar Mickey Mantle

Everybody knows that Casey Stengel has forgotten more baseball than I'll ever know. That's the trouble—he's forgotten it.

—Outfielder Jimmy Piersall, one of Stengel's Mets

The best way to test a Timex watch would be to strap it on his tongue.

—Umpire Marty Springstead on volatile manager Earl Weaver

I knew this spring when the Royals asked me if I wanted to take a stress test like the players, I said, "I don't need another one—I managed Ron Davis."

—Manager Billy Gardner

I've changed my mind about it. Instead of being bad, it stinks.

—Sparky Anderson, manager, on the designated hitter rule

Me and my owners think exactly alike. Whatever they're thinking, that's what I'm thinking.

—Jim Fregosi as manager of the Angels

I think early on in spring training we had a lot of good players. We didn't have a good team. And today I can make the statement that we've got a good team.

—Tigers manager Jim Leyland upon winning the 2006 pennant

When you win, you eat better, sleep better, and your beer tastes better. And your wife looks like Gina Lollobrigida.

—Red Sox skipper Johnny Pesky

What do managers really do? Worry. Constantly. For a living.

—Writer Leonard Koppett, from *A Thinking Man's Guide to Baseball*

"How you play the game" is for college boys. When you're playing for money, winning is the only thing that counts.

—Leo Durocher, manager

Nobody ever had enough of them.

—Manager Casey Stengel on pitchers

I like my players to be married and in debt. That's the way you motivate them.

—Ernie Banks, working with minor leaguers

We didn't sign Kenny Rogers [for the 2006 season] to babysit. We signed him because he was 59 games over .500. We brought him here because he can win games.

—Tigers manager Jim Leyland when asked if Rogers was signed to help a young pitching staff

It's not big if you look at it from the standpoint of the national debt.

—Twins manager Bill Rigney of his pitching staff's ERA

I believe in rules. Sure I do. If there weren't any rules, how could you break them?

—Leo Durocher, former player and manager

I can't tell how good a team really is until I see them playing under pressure.
—Manager Billy Martin

He [Mickey Mantle] thinks when I was born I was already sixty years old and had a wooden leg and came here to manage.
—Yankees skipper Casey Stengel

We're so bad right now that for us back-to-back home runs means one today and another one tomorrow.
—Orioles manager Earl Weaver

Go with the best you've got. A lot of people were talking about a matter of personalities, or that so-and-so's in the doghouse. To me, that's the most asinine statement that anybody could make.
—Manager Al Lopez

Despite all the nasty things I have said about umpires, I think they're 100 percent honest. But I can't for the life of me figure out how they arrive at some of their decisions.
—Manager Jimmy Dykes

The only thing I believe is this: a player does not have to like a manager and he does not have to respect a manager. All he has to do is obey the rules.

—Sparky Anderson, Reds manager

Baseball has been very good to me since I quit trying to play it.

—St. Louis manager Whitey Herzog

Billy Martin sent me up [to hit] for Al Kaline once. I made an out. I told him, "Keep doing this and you're going to get both of us run out of town."

—Tigers outfielder Gates Brown

One thing all managers hear that doesn't make sense at all is for the pitcher to say, "I ought to have a right to stay in and win or lose my own game." He doesn't have that right. It isn't his game.

—Astros manager Harry Walker

The first time Joe [Altobelli] said hello to some guys, he broke Earl Weaver's career record.

—Pitcher Jim Palmer contrasting two of his Orioles managers

The players make the manager; it's never the other way.

—Reds skipper Sparky Anderson

For five innings, it's the pitcher's game. After that, it's mine.

—Manager Fred Hutchinson

If you make a player feel like nothing, he'll play like nothing. I want them all coming to the park with the feeling that they have a chance to get in the game.

—Angels manager Gene Mauch

We have deep depth.

—Manager Yogi Berra

I'm not concerned about the other team stealing my signs. I'm just concerned about us getting them.

—Frank Howard as a minor league manager

When they ask you a question, answer it and just keep going. That way they can't ask you another one.

—Casey Stengel, manager, regarding sportswriters

Just give me twenty-five guys on the last year of their contract; I'll win the pennant every year.

—Manager Sparky Anderson

A manager who cannot get along with a .400 hitter ought to have his head examined.

—Manager Joe McCarthy on Ted Williams

There are three types of baseball players: those who make it happen, those who watch it happen, and those who wonder what happens.

—Dodgers manager Tommy Lasorda

The first guy who lays a finger on this blind old man is fined fifty bucks.

—Expos manager Gene Mauch to his team regarding an umpire he felt had just made a bad call

The toughest thing about managing is standing up for nine innings.

—Phillies manager Paul Owens

I come to play. I come to beat you. I come to kill you.

—Legendary manager Leo Durocher

The strategy part is overrated. Every manager tries to give his players the chance to be successful. Every manager I know knows that's the key.

—Jim Leyland, as the Pirates manager

I guess so, I've been fired three times.

—Dave Bristol after being asked if he considered himself to be a fiery manager

Percentage baseball must be good. If it weren't, it wouldn't work so often.

—Pinky Higgins, Red Sox manager

The two most important things in life are good friends and a strong bullpen.

—Manager Bob Lemon

It isn't every manager who's offered a multi-hour contract.

—Texas manager Connie Ryan

The pilgrims didn't have any experience when they first arrived here. Hell, if experience was that important, we'd never have had anybody walking on the moon.

—Managerial candidate Doug Rader

When I first became a manager, I asked Chuck [Tanner] for advice. He told me, "Always rent."

—Tony La Russa, as the White Sox manager

I gave Mike [Cuellar] more chances than I gave my first wife.

—Orioles skipper Earl Weaver

They say most good managers were mediocre players. I should be a helluva manager.

—Pitcher Charlie Hough

It never ends. You're only as good as the next game in this town [New York]. It never seems to be enough.

—Mets manager Willie Randolph, just prior to the 2006 playoffs, from *USA Today*

Team speed, team speed. Just give me some big [expletive] who can hit the ball out of the park.

—Earl Weaver, Orioles manager, on his preference for power over speed

Very few managers can remain when they're in ninth place unless they can tell a lot of jokes—and I can't tell a lot of jokes.

—White Sox manager Eddie Stanky

I'm not sure whether I'd rather be managing or testing bulletproof vests.

—Joe Torre, big-league manager

Football coaches walk across the field after the game and pretend to congratulate the opposing coach. Baseball managers head right for the beer.

—Writer Thomas Boswell

I never played by "the book" because I've never met the guy who wrote it.

—Dick Williams, Expos manager

A manager's job is simple. For 162 games, you try not to screw up all that smart stuff your organization did last December.

—Orioles manager Earl Weaver

If any of my players don't take a drink now and then they'll be gone. You don't play this game on ginger snaps.

—Controversial manager Leo Durocher

Just when my fellows learn to hit in this park [the Polo Grounds, first home of the Mets], they're gonna tear it down.

—Manager Casey Stengel

You have to improve your club if it means letting your own brother go.

—Joe McCarthy, manager of the Yankees

Cheating in baseball is just like hot dogs, french fries, and cold Cokes.

—Manager Billy Martin

I was probably as big a fan of the event as anyone else there. After all, I'd never seen anybody get 3,000 hits, either.

—Outfielder Lou Brock on attaining his 3,000th hit

I don't want to achieve immortality by making the Hall of Fame. I want to achieve immortality by not dying.

—Leo Durocher, manager, voted into the Hall posthumously

I believe managing is like holding a dove in your hand. If you hold it too tightly you kill it, but if you hold it too loosely, you lose it.

—Dodger manager Tommy Lasorda

I yelled from the dugout, "Watch the squeeze," and then I watched it [executed perfectly against his team].

—Manager Earl Weaver

When you're a professional, you come back no matter what happened the day before.

—Manager Billy Martin

The Yankees don't pay me to win every day—just two out of three.

—Manager Casey Stengel

Show me a good loser in professional sports and I'll show you an idiot. Show me a sportsman and I'll show you a player I'm looking to trade.

—Hall of Famer Leo Durocher

They say Lyndon Johnson can remember your name five years later. I might not know yours next week, but I can remember everything I ever saw a player do.

—Houston manager Grady Hatton

No matter how good you are, you're going to lose one-third of your games. No matter how bad you are, you're going to win one-third of your games. It's the other third that makes the difference.

—Dodger manager Tommy Lasorda

If we pitched as hard when we're not in trouble, we wouldn't get in trouble.

—Philosophy of manager Casey Stengel

I feel like a guy in an open casket at a funeral; everyone walks by and mumbles what a great guy you were, but you stay dead.

—Manager Tom Trebelhorn of all the condolences he received after being fired

Friendships are forgotten when the game begins.

—Alvin Dark, manager

It's what I hate most about this job. Monkeying around with people's lives is never fun. On the other hand, when I've picked the team, twenty-five players are monkeying around with my life.

—Manager Don Zimmer

Each year, new managers appear. And each season, the public response is "Who's he? Why him?" The fans never catch on. They want John Wayne and Humphrey Bogart. But they keep getting Jim Frey and Dick Howser.

—Writer Thomas Boswell, from *Inside Sports*

Man for man, we weren't a great team. We were an eighth-place team with [manager] George Stallings and without him we would have stayed there.

—Pitcher Bill James on the 1914 Miracle Braves

If it's true we learn by our mistakes, then Jim Frey will be the best manager ever.

—Umpire Ron Luciano

In playing or managing, the game of ball is only fun for me when I'm out in front and winning. I don't care a bag of peanuts for the rest of the game.

—New York Giants manager John McGraw

The team has shown me ways to lose I couldn't believe. You've got to look up and down the bench and say, "Can't anyone here play this game?"

—Casey Stengel, manager of the hapless Mets

A great manager has a knack for making ballplayers think they are better than they really are.

—Slugger Reggie Jackson

There are three things the average man thinks he can do better than anybody else: build a fire, run a hotel, and manage a baseball team.

—Minor league manager Rocky Bridges

The manager's toughest job is not calling the right play with the bases loaded and the score tied in an extra-inning game. It's telling a ballplayer that he's through, done, finished.

—Manager Jimmy Dykes

If the guys on the bench were as good as the guys you have out there [on the field], they'd be out there in the first place.

—Giants manager Frank Robinson

They say some of my stars drink whiskey, but I have found that the ones who drink milkshakes don't win many ballgames.

—Hall of Famer Casey Stengel

Managing a ball club is a job for which a man works, studies, hopes and, if he's gaited that way, prays—knowing all the time that if he gets it, he's bound, in the end, to be fired.

—Manager Birdie Tebbetts

In Los Angeles or San Francisco. I forget which.

—Pirates manager Danny Murtaugh, when asked where he thought his team would finish the season

The only clubhouse meetings I like are the ones dividing up playoff shares.

—Royals manager Billy Gardner

I don't know what I can tell you; you don't even drink.

—Bob Lemon, when asked for advice by young manager Don Kessinger

The worst thing about managing is the day you realize you want to win more than the players do.

—Manager Gene Mauch

Playing for Yogi [Berra] is like playing for your father. Playing for Billy [Martin] is like playing for your father-in-law.

—Designated hitter Don Baylor

A manager is like a fellow swimming in the ocean with a cut on his arm. Sooner or later the sharks are going to get him. Do you think I'm going to manage here [Texas] for twenty years? Hell, no.

—Eddie Stanky, just after being hired by the Rangers in 1977; he resigned after one day due to homesickness

Sometimes I look on Roy [Smalley] as my nephew, but sometimes only as my sister's son.

—Manager Gene Mauch of his relative/infielder

Everybody judges players different. I judge a player by what he does for his ballclub and not by what he does for himself.

—Manager Billy Martin

I'm probably the only guy who played for [Casey] Stengel before and after he was a genius.

—Hall of Famer Warren Spahn, who played under Stengel on the Boston Braves and on the New York Mets

We're about as important as the last player on the bench. That's just the way we get paid, too.

—Larry Dierker, Houston manager

I never questioned the integrity of an umpire. Their eyesight, yes.

—Hall of Fame manager Leo Durocher

Tommy [Lasorda] has a one-track mind and the traffic on it is very light.

—Dodger Steve Garvey on his manager

If you can say the morale of your club is good after losing ten out of twelve games, then your intelligence is a little low.

—Orioles manager Paul Richards

I'm basically a blue-collar-type manager that believes in a good work ethic, preparation, and a desire to win a baseball game.

—Manager Lou Piniella upon being hired as the new Cubs skipper for 2007

When you arrive at the ballpark and find your name has been scratched from the parking list.

—Manager Billy Martin on when one knows he's about to be fired

Keep them apart and keep the club.

—Manager Casey Stengel on players' wives

Believe what you want; no manager ever resigns.

—Manager Bucky Harris

Whew, I thought we would have to call the fire department, my team's so hot.

—Manager Casey Stengel

When we lost I couldn't sleep at night. When we win I can't sleep at night. But when you win, you wake up feeling better.

—Manager Joe Torre

I had my bad days on the field, but I didn't take them home with me. I left them in a bar along the way.

—Manager Bob Lemon

You talk about being recycled. Don Zimmer is the aluminum can of managing.

—Newspaper writer Tony Kornheiser

If you had to vote today [in 2006], you have to vote for Tony La Russa or Bobby Cox as one of the two greatest managers of all time.

—Ex-Tigers skipper Sparky Anderson

In this game of baseball, you live by the sword and die by it. You hit and get hit. Remember that.

—Alvin Dark, manager of the Indians, on knockdown and brushback pitches

Wayne [Comer], I think you're going to hit .290 this year, but you're going to be doing it in Montgomery, Alabama.

—Manager Mayo Smith of the Tigers

They say I have to get to know my players. That arithmetic is bad. Isn't it simpler for twenty-five of them to get to know me?

—Cleveland skipper Birdie Tebbetts

They [fly balls] don't bother us none. We're still working on grounders.

—Mets manager Casey Stengel, when asked if his team would work on handling fly balls under the tricky roof of the Astrodome

[Leo] Durocher played people, not colors.

—First baseman Bill White

Bad baseball players [retired from the game] make good managers.

—Orioles skipper Earl Weaver, who fit both descriptions; he was a poor player but a standout manager

Learn to know every man under you, get under his skin, know his faults. Then cater to him—with kindness or toughness as his case may demand.

—Manager John McGraw

CHAPTER SEVEN

Keys to Success

Many books have been written on how to succeed in business and a series of books offering tips on various topics for "idiots" fills bookshelves across the nation. In baseball, too, there are entire tomes devoted to success. Subtopics include everything from hitting, pitching, and fielding fundamentals to how a front office puts together a winner, to how a successful manager runs a team. Culling many of the words of wisdom from books, players, managers, coaches, team owners, ad infinitum, here now are some important quotations on the keys to baseball success.

While everyone can spout the lines about the key to baseball being pitching and/or three-run homers, the comments below offer a veritable diamond seminar. Further, since the game is made up of so many facets, going beyond the generalities of pitching and power, this chapter touches on many more aspects of baseball such as the art of base burglary. After all, one perks up his ears when, say, Maury Wills or Lou Brock speaks of larceny on the basepaths.

Likewise, an aspiring hitter must pay heed to the likes of Ted Williams when he spouts words of wisdom such as his idea of making sure one gets a good pitch to hit: "It means a ball that does not fool you, a ball that is not in a tough spot for you. Think of trying to hit it back up the middle. Try not to pull it every time."

Naturally, too, a pitching prospect listens aptly, *very* attentively, as Bob Gibson speaks of his craft and how he had disdain for waste pitches: "On an 0-and count, throw your best fastball or slider. Don't lay it in there when you've got 0-and-2 on the batter."

Some of the advice here is very general, as is true of Roger Clemens's terse "You have to strap it on and go get them." Other keys to success are quite specific such as Tom Seaver's "The good rising fastball is the best pitch in baseball." Still other quotations are rather philosophical in nature; consider Earl Weaver's famous line, "It's what you learn after you know it all that counts." Ted Turner, former owner of the Atlanta Braves, once summed up his idea of what it takes to win thusly, "What you've got to have in baseball is pitching, speed, and money." Finally, some keys don't even pertain to on-the-field facets, but instead concern intangible facets of baseball. As pitcher Andy Messersmith once put it, "Championships are won in the clubhouse."

So, here now is a crash course on success in the game of baseball.

Trade a player a year too early rather than a year too late.

—Baseball executive Branch Rickey

The team that wins two-thirds of its one-run games usually wins the pennant.

—Cincinnati's Pete Rose

The fundamentals have never changed, even since the days of Babe Ruth. They did the same things that the hitters today do mechanically to get in a good hitting position, to recognize pitch, location and then trust their eyes to tell their hands whether to react or not.

—Hitting coach Rudy Jaramillo, from *Hitting Secrets of the Pros* by Wayne Stewart

Winning isn't everything. Wanting to win is.

—Pitcher Catfish Hunter

I was told by a very smart man a long time ago that talent always beats experience. Because by the time you get experience, the talent's gone.

—Philadelphia Phillies manager Pat Corrales

We [the Twins] just do what T.K. [manager Tom Kelly] tells us. Don't get too high or too low. Just go out, give 100 percent and we'll win the battle one game at a time.

—Minnesota star Kirby Puckett

Be relaxed, don't wave the bat, don't clench it. Be ready to hit down with the barrel of the bat. Just swing it and let the weight drive the ball.

—Pirates outfield great Paul Waner

Success has no shortcut, only a high price of pain and humiliation. Baseball requires mental strength.

—Carlton Fisk

Never the same pitch twice, never the same place twice, never the same speed twice.

—Pitcher Ed Lopat's tips on pitching success

It's like most anything. If you want to be a loser, there's always a way to dwell on the negative. If you want to win, there's always a way to think positively.

—Manager Tony La Russa

Just putting on a Yankee uniform gave me a little confidence, I think. That club could carry you. You were better than you actually were.

—Yankees shortstop Mark Koenig

There's a lot of muscle memory involved [in throwing strikes] and a lot of mechanics are involved in it—you just gotta get to that certain slot.

—Pitcher Matt Mantei, from *Pitching Secrets of the Pros* by Wayne Stewart

A manager wins games in December. He tries not to lose them in July. You win pennants in the offseason when you build your teams with trades and free agents.

—Orioles manager Earl Weaver

A lot of successful teams take their first step down when they become satisfied with their success rather than constantly moving forward. When they forget how they got to the top they lose what it takes to stay there.

—Sportswriter Craig R. Wright

Stand your ground and take your lumps.

—Advice of catcher Yogi Berra

To pitch to every batter as though I were facing his the first time. That helps make you careful.

—Pitcher Whit Wyatt's rule he devised for himself

You hit home runs not by chance, but by preparation.

—Yankees slugger Roger Maris

Hey, if a guy's got eight years in the big leagues and less than twenty homers, thinking home run is not a very smart move.

—Infielder Alan Bannister, when asked if he went to the plate thinking home run, from *The Sporting News*, August 1, 1983

When you steal a base, 99 percent of the time you steal on a pitcher. You actually never steal on a catcher.

—Former stolen base king Lou Brock

To hit .400 you need a great start and you can't have a slump. The year I did it, I was around .410, .412 all season and I was really hitting the ball on the nose. Hitting is a business. With two strikes, you really protect that plate.

—Standout first baseman Bill Terry

You call that [diligent preparation] natural? I swung a 44-ounce bat 600 times a night, 4,200 times a week, 47,200 swings every winter. Wrists. The fastball's by you. You gotta wrist it out. Forty-seven thousand two hundred times.

—Dodgers outfielder George Shuba, from *The Boys of Summer* by Roger Kahn

Many people resented my impatience and honesty, but I never cared about acceptance as much as I cared about respect.

—Dodgers star Jackie Robinson

I know five reasons why he isn't gong to beat me out—my wife and four children.

—Infielder Willie Miranda on a player trying to take his spot on the roster

The best advice I can give you is . . . Practice, practice, practice. . . . And when you think you're good enough, practice some more. . . . And then, when you think you're as good as you can be, practice some more.

—300-game winner Phil Niekro, from *Tales from the Ballpark* by Mike Shannon

Never swing at a ball you're fooled on or have trouble hitting.

—Batting tip from outfielder Ted Williams

In baseball, there's no such thing as a small enemy.

—Pitcher Fernando Valenzuela

When we were challenged, when we had to win, we stuck together and played with a fury and determination that could only come from team spirit. We had a pride in our performance that was very real. It took on the form of snobbery.

—Yankees pitcher Waite Hoyt

Win any way you can, so long as you can get away with it.

—Leo Durocher, longtime big-league manager

It's a simple game. It's the same game that our dads and moms taught us in the backyards: "Play! Catch the ball. See the ball. Hit it. Make a good throw."

—Baltimore coach Elrod Hendricks

Power should never be used. The manager who uses power has lost control. Common sense—that's the key.

—Manager Sparky Anderson

Hitting is a summation of internal forces. It's everything. It's not just hands or wrists. You have to get the whole body into it.

—Coach Jim Lefebvre, from *Men at Work* by George F. Will

Old-timers say over and over that players nowadays don't talk baseball. What they really mean is [talking baseball after a game] in a bar. Modern players don't want to sit around a bar. They're more into conditioning; more sophisticated about health.

—Sam McDowell, Indians pitcher, from *Indians on the Game* by Wayne Stewart

Losing is no disgrace if you've given your best.

—Hall of Famer Jim Palmer

I'm looking for a ballplayer with enough guts not to fight back.

—Brooklyn executive Branch Rickey on the key to Jackie Robinson, signed as the first African American player, after Robinson had asked Rickey if he was looking for "a Negro who is afraid to fight back."

Creating success is tough, but keeping it is tougher. You have to keep producing, you can't ever stop.

—Phillies infielder Pete Rose

After two strikes, concede the long ball to the pitcher; shorten up on the bat and try to put the head of the bat on the ball.

—Boston's superstar Ted Williams

Most pitchers deliberately alter their pattern of pitching when a game is not on the line. Why show a hitter your best stuff when the game is out of reach?

—Pitching coach Roger Craig

Our greatest chance, I believe, lies in the fact that we will finish the season at home. The encouragement of a friendly big city is no small factor in a team's success.

—Pitcher Christy Mathewson

I'm the kind of guy who doesn't let up. If I've got you bleeding in six or seven different places, I'll make sure you're bleeding in eight or nine.

—Pitcher Dave Stewart

The difference between the old ballplayer and the new ballplayer is the jersey. The old ballplayer cared about the name on the front. The new ballplayer cares about the name on the back.

—Star first baseman Steve Garvey, from *Baseball and the Meaning of Life*, edited by Josh Leventhal

I am the best. That's my belief. If people think I'm cocky, it's just because I'm highly competitive. It's one of the things I need to feel to keep my edge.

—Pitcher Frank Tanana

I owe my success to expansion pitching, a short right-field fence, and my hollow bats.

—Tigers star Norm Cash, known to have corked his bat

I stopped thinking as though every trip to the plate was a life-or-death proposition. Instead of thinking I had to hit every pitch with every ounce of strength, I tried to pick out a good pitch and swing naturally.

—Phillies star Mike Schmidt to *Pennsylvania Heritage, from Baseball Digest*, December 2006

You can't push young people. They shouldn't have pressure on them to do it yet.

—Manager Sparky Anderson on grooming young players

I loved to play catch and play ball and I played every chance I could. I played on street teams and in the Buffalo Twilight League, the American Legion, city municipal. I was always playing ball and always thinking about playing ball.

—Hall of Fame pitcher Warren Spahn, from *The Head Game* by Roger Kahn

You cannot have a misstep in the major leagues. If you stumble, if you hesitate, if you stop to look instead of just picking up the third-base coach, you'll be out. Those outfielders and the guys who make the relay throws are the best in the world.

—Indians announcer Matt Underwood on the key to scoring from second on a hit

What you've got to have in baseball is pitching, speed, and money.

—Atlanta Braves owner Ted Turner

You can't fear failure and you can't fear success.

—Relief pitcher Paul Shuey from the *Plain Dealer*, September 21, 2000

To hit .400 you've got to have power to keep the defense back and spread out. And you've got to be fast.

—Ted Williams, Hall of Famer

I like to feel nasty and grubby. I'm not out there to win a beauty contest. I'm out there to be mean and win, not make friends.

—Outfielder Kirk Gibson, with the Detroit Tigers in 1984

On an 0-and-2 count, throw your best fastball or slider. Don't lay it in there when you've got 0-and-2 on the batter.

—Bob Gibson on one of his keys to success

[Hank] Greenberg made a great hitter out of himself. He did it by constant practice. . . . He'd stay after games and hit until darkness made him quit.

—Manager Paul Richards

What does that [getting a good ball to hit] mean? It means a ball that does not fool you, a ball that is not in a tough spot for you. Think of trying to hit it back up the middle. Try not to pull it every time.

—Outfielder Ted Williams

He had that fear that the great ones have. He had that fear of failure and I think he tried to minimize that possibility by working to make sure all margin for error was eliminated.

—Cubs manager Jim Frey on Hall of Famer Ryne Sandberg

Throw strikes. Home plate don't move.

—Pitcher Satchel Paige

If you play an aggressive, hustling game, it forces your opponents into errors.

—Pete Rose, all-time hit king

You should do everything possible to win short of scratching the other guy's eyes out.

—Manager Ken Aspromonte

Keep those nits and gnats [light hitters] off the base, cause those lions and tigers will get ya.

—Catcher Sam Narron

The names change, but the Dodgers' tradition remains forever.

—Dodgers manager Tommy Lasorda

In the majors, the physical part of the game is over—it becomes mental. Baseball is a game of adjustments. Those who make adjustments are a success.

—Cy Young winner Rick Sutcliffe, from *Indians on the Game* by Wayne Stewart

When you're a winner you're always happy, but if you're happy as a loser you'll always be a loser.

—Colorful Tigers pitcher Mark Fidrych

Winning depends on where you put your priorities. It's usually best to put them over the fence.

—Slugger Jason Giambi

I wanted to beat [my peers] in every department. Fielding, hitting, running the bases. I played that game all my life and it kept me on my toes.

—Braves great Eddie Mathews

A good basestealer should make the whole infield jumpy. Whether you steal or not, you're changing the rhythm of the game.

—Joe Morgan, Hall of Famer

Twenty-five players, one heartbeat.

—Marlins manager Jim Leyland on what it takes for success

Great pitchers demonstrate composure, pride, and competitive instincts. They don't allow trivial things to upset them.

—Pitching coach Roger Craig

The more you can let the ball get to you and still hit it out front, the better you'll be. We always say, "Stay back until you're ready to attack it."

—Hitting coach Rudy Jaramillo, from *Hitting Secrets of the Pros* by Wayne Stewart

The trick against [Don] Drysdale is to hit him before he hits you.

—First baseman Orlando Cepeda

Playing baseball is much easier if everyone thinks you're an off-the-wall babbling idiot.

—Pitcher Jim Kern

Being patient, also being able to hit with two strikes. I think you have to be comfortable hitting with two strikes as a lead-off hitter.

—Outfielder Rickey Henderson's keys to success, from *Hitting Secrets of the Pros* by Wayne Stewart

I don't know it there's anything in this world or any world that makes McRae afraid.

—Hitting coach Charlie Lau on Royals star Hal McRae's winning attitude

There's a certain scent when you get close to winning. You may go a long time without winning, but you never forget that scent.

—Kansas City pitcher Steve Busby

In order to be an outstanding baserunner, you have to eliminate the fear of failure. It's like being a safecracker.

—Dodger shortstop Maury Wills

Speed is a great asset; but it's greater when it's combined with quickness—and there's a big difference.

—Tigers great Ty Cobb

Every time you learn something, it helps you—maybe a week, a month, maybe a year from now. Once you stop learning—let me tell you—you're going to be in the second row looking at somebody else playing.

—Hall of Fame pitcher Fergie Jenkins

In this game, your attitude determines your altitude.

—Manager Jack McKeon

Progress always involves risks. You can't steal second bases and keep your foot on first.

—Writer Frederick B. Wilcox

When he went 0-for-4 and we lost, he could bite off the head of a rattlesnake. When he went 0-for-4 and we won, he ran around the clubhouse like he had hit two grand slams and stole the mustard off somebody's hot dog.

—Tigers manager Sparky Anderson on Kirk Gibson being a consummate team player

I tell them to do what feels comfortable to you, whether it's choking up, spreading your feet out, thinking of going the other way, or being a little more aggressive in the zone. Now, if he doesn't have success, well, then we have to make an adjustment.

—Keys to success for two-strike hitting, from hitting coach Rudy Jaramillo, from *Hitting Secrets of the Pros* by Wayne Stewart

A win in April is just as important as a win in September.

—Reds manager Dave Bristol

In baseball, my theory is to strive for consistency, not to worry about the "numbers." If you dwell on statistics, you get shortsighted; if you aim for consistency, the numbers will be there at the end.

—Hall of Fame pitcher Tom Seaver

When a team gives us an extra out, we [Yankees] jump on them. It's like chum in the water and our guys can smell it. Then they get after it. We go into our attack mode.

—Pitcher Roger Clemens

When I get to first I figure second and third will be mine in just a second or two.

—Speedy Royals outfielder Willie Wilson on the confidence needed to succeed

I guess I was never much in awe of anybody. I think you have to have that attitude if you're going to go far in this game.

—Hall of Fame pitcher Bob Gibson of the St. Louis Cardinals

I want to be known as a good major leaguer and good major leaguers work to become good.

—Third baseman Alex Rodriguez, from *www.baseballalmanac.com*

Statistics are overrated. Championships are won in the clubhouse.

—Pitcher Andy Messersmith

When the leaves turn brown, I'll wear the batting crown.

—Pirate outfielder and two-time batting champ Dave Parker on confidence

We've tried both [three- and four-man rotations] and didn't have any success with the three-man. We got by on the old adage, "Whatever gets you there." It's not good to be overly cute in the postseason.

—A's general manager Billy Beane as Oakland entered the 2006 playoffs, from *USA Today Sports Weekly*

What you're thinking, what shape your mind is in, is what makes the biggest difference of all.

—Hall of Famer Willie Mays

A great ballplayer is a player who will take a chance.

—Baseball executive Branch Rickey

They're not the greatest ballclub I've ever seen, but they think they are.

—Cleveland manager Joe Gordon on his team

[Batting] . . . is a study in psychology, a sizing up of pitcher and catcher and observing little details that are of immense importance.

—Hall of Famer Ty Cobb

If James Brown is the "Godfather of Soul," [Bill] Veeck was the "Godfather of the Diamond." He was a little irreverent; he had fun. Everything he did had heart. Now baseball takes itself too seriously. We've got a lot of "suits" in the game who have the passion of a mackerel.

—Veeck's son Mike on a key to rejuvenating fan interest in baseball

There are two important things to remember. Keep in shape and know where each pitch is going. It pays off. I knew where my pitches were going because I worked on control continuously.

—Pitching star Red Ruffing

CHAPTER EIGHT

The World Series

It has been called both the Fall and the Autumnal Classic and this series of crucial games, the true granddaddy of championship sporting events in the United States, has been around, uninterrupted save two times, since 1903 when the Pittsburgh Pirates lost to the Boston franchise then known as the Americans. The first contest of the event, then called "the Championship of the United States," was held at Boston's Huntington Avenue Grounds, as was the finale, a game witnessed by only 7,455 fans. Back then, by the way, it was a best-of-nine series, and *this* Boston crew stormed back from a deficit of one win to Pittsburgh's three, taking the final four games, a bit like the back-to-the-wall Boston Red Sox of 2004 in their playoff versus the Yankees.

Some of the World Series have been duds, and four-game sweeps tend to leave little room for dramatics. Fortunately, though, the pyrotechnics and the tension of moments such as Pittsburgh's win behind Bill Mazeroski's ultimate walk-off home run versus the Yanks in 1960 (or Joe Carter's three-run, Series-ending homer off Mitch Williams for the Toronto Blue Jays in 1993) provide lasting thrills.

On the other side of the coin, the pitching realm, there have been classic matchups such as the 1968 duel between Detroit Tiger's Mickey Lolich and St. Louis Cardinals ace Bob Gibson. Both men entered the seventh game with a 2–0 slate and both threw shutout ball through the first six frames before Gibson blinked and Lolich, on two days' rest, won to become one of a handful of pitchers to nail down three Series games. Of course, the ultimate in pitching perfection for an entire Series (no disrespect meant for Don Larsen's perfect game in 1956) came way back in 1905 when Christy Mathewson of the New York Giants not only notched three wins, but did so by firing three shutouts. That's good for an invisible ERA of 0.00 over 27 innings with 18 K's (versus

only one walk) to boot as he held the Philadelphia Athletics to an average of five baserunners per game.

It's only natural, then, that this event has led to some great quotations as well. It's time now to relive those words.

We're here to prove there is no Santa Claus.

—Orioles great Brooks Robinson at the start of the 1969 World Series, figuring his O's would stop the "Miracle Mets."

They say anything can happen in a short series. I just didn't expect it to be that short.

—Manager Al Lopez on his 1954 Indians being swept by the Giants

We turned it on as soon as the playoffs started. I don't know how. I don't care.

—Cardinals third baseman Scott Rolen after winning the 2006 World Series

Well, it's like when I go to a dance. I always go home with the guy who brought me.

—Manager Bob Lemon on why he started Ed Figueroa in the 1978 World Series

I can't remember the last time I missed a ground ball. I'll remember that one.

—Boston's Bill Buckner on his infamous error in Game Six of the 1986 World Series, allowing the ball to scoot through his legs at first base

They played two World Series games at the Polo Grounds this afternoon—the one I watched and the one broadcast by Graham McNamee.

—Sportswriter Ring Lardner, 1922 World Series

Club officials apparently believe that I can live for a year on fruit and vegetables which thoughtful Detroit fans contributed during the last game of the World Series.

—Outfielder Joe Medwick alluding to fans who had pelted him with objects during the 1934 World Series

I'll tell you what, we're having an earth . . .

—Television announcer Al Michaels cut off in mid-sentence due to the earthquake before Game Two of the 1989 World Series

What does a mama bear on the pill have in common with the World Series? No cubs.

—Cubs announcer Harry Caray

If them guys [the Tigers] are thinking, they're as good as licked right now.

—Cardinals pitcher Dizzy Dean before the 1934 World Series which St. Louis did win in seven contests

Those of us who were there will remember it, surely, as long as we have any baseball memory and those who wanted to be there and were not will always be sorry.

—On Game Six of the 1975 World Series, when Carlton Fisk hit his "body English" homer from "Game Six, Game Six" by Roger Angell in *Five Seasons*, reprinted in *The Baseball Reader* by Charles Einstein

If you do everything right, you'll still lose 40 percent of your games—but you'll also end up in the World Series.

—Writer Thomas Boswell

We are part of history. We are something special. We were playing for more than the World Series. Now we have some bragging rights.

—Yankees outfielder Bernie Williams after winning the 2000 Series versus crosstown rivals, the Mets

I done it for the wife and kiddies.

—White Sox pitcher Eddie Cicotte on why he fixed the 1919 World Series

If I'd have known his head was there, I would have thrown the ball harder.

—The Detroit Tigers shortstop whose throw struck Dizzy Dean on his forehead, 1934 World Series

So far as I know, they haven't changed the World Series rules. This thing still goes to the team that wins four games and not to the club that makes the most records.

—Pirates manager Danny Murtaugh after Game Six of the 1960 World Series, tied, but dominated statistically by the Yankees, from *And the Crowd Goes Wild* by Joe Garner

The longest out and the shortest home run of the season beat us.

—Cleveland manager Al Lopez on the amazing Willie Mays catch and a "cheap" Dusty Rhodes homer in the 1954 World Series, from *And the Fans Roared* by Joe Garner

The World Series is different and you must play the game different. You got to have that mental tenaciousness . . . you got to rise to the occasion . . . to put it bluntly, you've got to have the killer instinct to be a World Series hero.

—Outfielder Reggie Jackson, from *Out-of-Left-Field Baseball Trivia* by Robert Obojski and Wayne Stewart

You create your own momentum. You just have to approach every game like it's the last game you're going to play.

—Mets first baseman Carlos Delgado during the 2006 National League Championship Series

That first World Series finished baseball as a sport. Afterwards the owners and later the ballplayers became big-time businessmen.

—Sportswriter John R. Tunis, quoted in *The Head Game* by Roger Kahn

Miracle, my eye.

—Mets pitcher Tom Seaver dismissing claims that it took a miracle for his team to win it all in 1969

Tied.

—Pitcher Bill Lee, when asked how he would characterize the 1975 World Series up to the point of Lee's interview

We needed an unexpected move. Had Ruth made the steal, it would have been declared the smartest piece of baseball in the history of World Series play.

—Yankees manager Miller Huggins on Ruth's attempted steal of second to end the 1926 World Series, from *The Big Bam* by Leigh Montville

The minute I think any one of you ain't playing ball to win—if I think you're laying down—I'm gonna pull you out even if I have to make an infielder out of a bullpen catcher.

—White Sox manager Kid Gleason, during the fixed 1919 World Series, from *Eight Men Out* by Eliot Asinof

It's never happened in the World Series competition and it still hasn't.

—Catcher Yogi Berra on Don Larsen's perfect game

He's not at his locker yet, but four guys are over there interviewing his glove.

—Former pitcher Rex Barney on Orioles star Brooks Robinson after the 1970 World Series

We're spending all our money to try to solve the problems in the Middle East. We ought to be spending it on educating these idiots here.

—Outfielder Reggie Smith on unruly Yankees fans, World Series of 1978

It's like the Fourth of July, New Year's Eve, and your birthday all wrapped in one.

—Pitcher Tom Seaver on the feel of the World Series

Until now, the only sport I associated with I-70 was bingo.

—Writer Joe Gilmartin on the St. Louis versus Kansas City "I-70" World Series

When we played, World Series checks meant something. Now all they do is screw up your taxes.

—Dodgers pitcher Don Drysdale

I don't want to be one of those great players who never made the Series.

—Outfielder Rickey Henderson on being traded to the Yankees

About thirty minutes after the last out, I saw Bob Gibson in my office and he said, "Welcome to the club." When you're around here [the Cardinals], you don't feel you can join the club until you win the World Series.

—St. Louis manager Tony La Russa after the 2006 Series, from *USA Today Sports Weekly*

Do you choke on your [expletive] microphone?

—An irate Casey Stengel to a reporter who had just asked him if his Yankees had choked after losing the 1957 World Series to the Braves

We're the best team in baseball—but not by much.

—Reds manager Sparky Anderson after the 1975 World Series versus Boston

I don't think you play this game for any other reason than to get to the World Series. I've thought about it since Little League, when you dream of hitting that home run in the ninth inning.

—Slugger Ken Griffey Jr.

Wow, man, I don't know who'll win this, but isn't it great just to be here?

—All-time hits leader Pete Rose to catcher Carlton Fisk during the 11th inning of Game Six of the 1975 World Series, many experts' pick as the greatest Series game ever, from *The Image of Their Greatness* by Lawrence Ritter and Donald Honig

He did it with a tremendous assortment of pitches that seemed to have five forward speeds, including a slow one that ought to have been equipped with backup lights.

—Sportswriter Shirley Povich on Don Larsen's perfect game in the 1956 World Series

Game 7, no way you can say what anybody is going to do. It's an out-of-body experience.

—Mets general manager Omar Minaya, in 2006, on postseason play, from the Associated Press

There were fifty-five reasons why I shouldn't have pitched him [Ed Lopat], but fifty-six why I should.

—Yankees manager Casey Stengel on his Game Seven pitcher in the 1952 World Series

To do that to [sweep] a ball club as good as the Dodgers is almost unthinkable. I'm just glad I was here to see it.

—Orioles third baseman Brooks Robinson of the 1966 World Series, from *The History of the Baltimore Orioles* by John Nichols

I had two great thrills in the World Series—when I thought it was over and then when it actually was over.

—Pitcher Sandy Koufax on the climax of the 1963 World Series

I was pitching strictly on adrenaline. You put being tired out of your mind. You don't think about that stuff. There's no need for a pitcher to do that during the regular season.

—Pitcher Randy Johnson of his stints in Games Six and Seven in the World Series of 2001

We are never too old or too bothered to see ourselves wrapping up a World Series victory with a homer in the final inning of the seventh game.

—Writer Ron Fimrite

If the World Series goes seven games, it will be NBC's longest-running show this fall.

—TV host Johnny Carson, from *Sports Illustrated*

It was definitely a day for the hitters. Almost like slow-pitch softball: everybody hits!

—Yankee pitcher Ralph Terry on the 1960 World Series slugfest in Game Seven, from *The Seventh Game* by Barry Levenson

If I can get the Philadelphia Phillies to win the World Series after a hundred years, then I can do anything.

—Phillies star Pete Rose of the 1980 World Series

No other sporting event can compare with a good Series. The Super Bowl is a three-hour interruption in a week of drink and Rotarian parties.

—Writer Roger Kahn, from *Sport*

No, why should I?

—Yankee pitcher Don Larsen, when asked if he tires of talking about his World Series perfect game

This World Series [2006] is turning out to be, in so many ways, like a Hollywood story. I don't know what the outcome is going to be, but I am sure hearts are going to be broken like in the movies.

—Tigers coach Andy Van Slyke, from *USA Today Sports Weekly*

Where else would you want to be in October, except here?

—Yankees shortstop Derek Jeter on the World Series

I guess the biggest thrill I had was crouching behind the plate, giving signals when Ted Williams was the hitter. I didn't know whether to call the pitch or get his autograph.

—Catcher Joe Garagiola of the Cardinals on the World Series of 1946

Even when your grandkids have grandkids, nobody will win it the way we did in '85 . . . That was a team that got pushed right up against the wall and, somehow, the wall moved.

—Royals third baseman George Brett

You kind of took it for granted around the Yankees that there was always going to be baseball in October.

—Yankees great Whitey Ford

I want a new catcher. If somebody's going to set a record for passed balls in the World Series, I don't want it to be me.

—New York Giants catcher Wes Westrum after having difficulty handling knuckleball hurler Hoyt Wilhelm during the 1954 World Series

I didn't come up here to read.

—Hank Aaron to Yankee catcher Yogi Berra during the World Series after Berra told him the right way to hold his bat was with the trademark where he could read it (also listed as "I came up here to hit, not to read.")

[Willie Mays] then whirled and threw, like some olden statue of a Greek javelin hurler. As he threw, off came the cap and then Mays himself continued to spin around after the gigantic effort of returning the ball . . . He went down flat on his belly and out of sight.

—Author Arnold Hano, from his book *A Day in the Bleachers*

To me, baseball is as honorable as any other business. It has to be, or it would not last out a season . . . Crookedness and baseball do not mix . . . This year, 1919, is the greatest season of them all.

—White Sox owner Charles A. Comiskey, ironic words in light of the discovery that his team threw the World Series that season, quoted by his biographer G. W. Axelson, from *Eight Men Out* by Eliot Asinof

After watching Roger Clemens hit in the World Series, I know this is one award he'll never win.

—Slugger Don Baylor after winning the award for the top designated hitter

When I was younger, yes.

—Pirates manager Danny Murtaugh, when asked on his birthday if he could come up with a better wish than winning the Series

There is no script.

—Cardinals manager Tony La Russa on the unpredictability of World Series play, from the Associated Press

I believe he [Christy Mathewson] could have continued to pitch shutouts until Christmas.

—Writer Grantland Rice on Mathewson's three complete-game shutouts in the 1905 Series

They can't come back. The doors are closed to them for good. The most scandalous chapter in the game's history is closed.

—Baseball commissioner Kenesaw Mountain Landis, banning the eight White Sox players who threw the 1919 World Series

Tighter than a bullfighter's pants.

—Outfielder Tommy Holmes on Duke Snider in his first World Series ever

The imperfect man pitched a perfect game yesterday.

—*New York Daily News* writer Joe Trimble on Don Larsen's Series perfecto in 1956

When you get the opportunity to win a World Series, you have to look at it as your only chance.

—Mets closer Billy Wagner in 2006

It is the fat men against the tall men at the annual office picnic.

—Sportswriter Frank Graham on the sloppiness of the 1945 World Series

It's still kind of amazing what four games can do for your career.

—1998 World Series MVP Scott Brosius on his success and fame, from *USA Today Sports Weekly*

Gimme the [g.d.] ball and get the hell out of here.

—Yankees pitcher Vic Raschi to Yogi Berra, who was trying to talk to his pitcher during a key moment in the 1949 World Series

You have to understand how difficult it is. There are so many variables. You need talent, breaks, timing, and luck. You just try not to set yourself up too high to get disappointed.

—Catcher Mike Piazza on winning in postseason play, from *USA Today*

You couldn't be Jewish, too?

—Dodgers manager Walt Alston to pitcher Don Drysdale, who had started Game One of the 1965 World Series (and was bombed, lifted in the third inning) over Jewish pitcher Sandy Koufax, who was observing Yom Kippur that day and would therefore not pitch

I'm coming down [stealing second] on the next pitch, Krauthead.

—Volatile outfielder Ty Cobb to shortstop Honus Wagner

As the ball left the bat, I said to myself two things. The first thing I said was, "Hello, double." The second thing I said was, "Oh, [expletive], he's out there."

—Yankees third baseman Clete Boyer of Willie Mays, from the 1962 World Series

Baseball is really two sports—the summer game and the autumn game. One is the leisurely pastime of our national mythology. The other is not so gentle.

—Writer Thomas Boswell from *How Life Imitates the World Series*

I remember coming out on the field and seeing the snow. They were playing Jingle Bells on the PA system.

—Manager Jim Leyland on Game Four of the 1997 World Series—the coldest game in Series history—with his Marlins playing in frigid Cleveland

Fred, I'm going to hit one off the wall. Drive me in.

—Boston catcher Carlton Fisk to teammate Fred Lynn moments before Fisk connected on his famous "body English" home run during Game Six of the 1975 World Series

I love facing people that haven't seen me before. No matter if they have scouting reports or not, it's still different when you get out there.

—Tigers pitcher Kenny Rogers on the 2006 World Series

One day we were the laughingstock of baseball and the next we were champions.

—First baseman Ed Kranepool on his "Miracle Mets" of '69

The mark of a team isn't winning the championship; it's how you defend the championship.

—Yankees owner George Steinbrenner

My idea of the height of conceit would be a political speaker that would go on the air when the World Series is on.

—Humorist Will Rogers

The only stage I need is the World Series.

—Three-time MVP Alex Rodriguez, from *www.baseballalmanac.com*

Too much spit on it.

—Dodgers pitcher Billy Loes, when asked why he balked in the 1952 World Series

He would throw one so lazy, so soft, so absolutely devoid of stuff, that a handwriting expert sitting in the stands could have read Ford Frick's character from his signature on the ball.

—Sportswriter George Kirksey on Dizzy Dean's pitches in the 1938 World Series

I looked into his eyes and saw that they were bloodshot, but they weren't foggy. I gave him the ball and told him to get [Tony] Lazerri.

—Cardinals manager Rogers Hornsby, who used a hungover Grover Cleveland Alexander to nail down the seventh game of the 1926 World Series

Maybe God can do something about such a play; man cannot.

—Yanks manager Casey Stengel on outfielder Bill Virdon's stunning catch in the 1960 World Series

Pressure? Well, it ain't hitting in forty-four straight games because I did that and it was fun. The playoffs are pressure.

—All-time hit king Pete Rose

You can't just turn it on, like a switch.

—Yankees second baseman Chuck Knoblauch in 2000, on teams that cruise into the World Series then need to kick it up once more

When Michael Jordan has dunked for the 12th time in a basketball game, it gets boring. When [5'6"] Spud Webb dunks for the first time, everybody thinks it's the best dunk of the season. The Tigers just dunked for the first time in a while.

—Detroit coach Andy Van Slyke on the thrill of the Tigers surprising success, making it to the World Series in 2006, from *USA Today Sports Weekly*

The balls aren't the same balls, the bats aren't the same length, and it's further between the bases.

—Outfielder Reggie Jackson on the pressure of the World Series

I think we shocked the world.

—Outfielder Jim Edmonds on his Cardinals' record for the fewest regular season wins ever, 83, by a Series-winning team

When you're the butt of everybody's jokes and you're the opening line on Jay Leno and [Dave] Letterman for so long, this feels pretty good.

—Tigers pitcher Todd Jones, prior to the start of the 2006 World Series, from *www.mlb.com*

When I came here [to the Yankees], I was told there's two seasons: regular season and postseason. There's not too many teams I've played for who expect to get to the postseason. This team has been there enough that they expect to get to the postseason every year.

—Pitcher Randy Johnson

Team spirit doesn't apply here. This isn't the College World Series. With 27,000 bucks on the line, I hate everybody.

—A's pitcher Ken Holtzman of the 1974 World Series

The gods decree a heavyweight match only once in a while and a national election only every four years, but there is a World Series with every revolution of the earth around the sun. And in between, what varied pleasure long drawn out!

—Writer Jacques Barzun in *God's Country and Mine*, from *The Baseball Reader* by Charles Einstein

That problem is, uh, behind me now.

—Royals star George Brett after surgery corrected his hemorrhoid problem that developed during the 1980 World Series

I turned my back and ran, looked over my shoulder once to gauge the flight of the ball, then kept running. I caught it the way a football end catches a long leading pass. Then I spun and threw.

—Giants center fielder Willie Mays, recapping his famous catch of a drive hit by Vic Wertz in the 1954 World Series

If this damned thing doesn't start soon, I'm going to fly straight up into the air.

—Orioles outfielder Curt Blefary, prior to the start of the 1966 World Series

The only reason I don't like playing in the World Series is I can't watch myself play.

—Outfielder Reggie Jackson

[Joe] DiMaggio could have done all his hitting in a chimney.

—Writer Arthur Baer on DiMaggio's popping up four straight times to the catcher to open the 1950 World Series

The last time the Cubs won a World Series was in 1908. The last time they were in one was 1945. Hey, any team can have a bad century.

—Cubs manager Tom Trebelhorn

I don't think either team is capable of winning.

—Sportswriter Warren Brown on the Tigers and Cubs in the 1945 World Series (also listed as, "I don't see how either team can possibly win.")

It's like the Kennedy assassination. Everyone I see comes up and tells me where they were and what they were doing when [Kirk] Gibson hit that home run.

—Reliever Dennis Eckersley, who dished up Gibson's dramatic Game One pinch-hit homer in the 1988 Series

Eighty-six years of "waiting till next year," and then to have it come to fruition, was something special, long beyond people's expectations.

—Hall of Fame catcher Carlton Fisk on the Red Sox' Series win in 2004

I'm just happy I got out of that bloodbath without actual physical abuse.

—Pitcher Al Leiter of Toronto on a 15–14 win in the 1993 World Series

Just because we have done it a few times, it doesn't mean it is an easy thing to do. The best teams make it to the playoffs, but it is the hottest team that wins it. A team has to be hot at the right time.

—Yankees shortstop Derek Jeter prior to the 2006 playoffs, from *USA Today*

I threw it in and the Yankees laid on it.

—Pitcher Barney Schultz of the Cards on his "mattress pitch" in the 1964 World Series

World Series week indicates that baseball is one of America's major disturbances.

—Sportswriter Arthur Baer

I'm forever blowing ballgames . . .

—Sportswriter Ring Lardner, singing a parody of *I'm Forever Blowing Bubbles*, with his lyrics aimed at the Chicago Black Sox of 1919

I never considered taking him out. I had a commitment to his heart.

—St. Louis Cardinals manager Johnny Keane of his sticking with pitching ace Bob Gibson to wrap up the finale of the 1964 World Series, even though Gibson was, by his standards, a bit shaky that day, giving up five runs in a win over the Yankees

No matter how long you have been playing, you still get butterflies before the big one.

—Brooklyn's Pee Wee Reese on the World Series

It's the same as any other ballgame you'll remember as long as you live.

—Catcher Joe Garagiola on World Series play

The Ruth is mighty and shall prevail.

—Sportswriter Heywood Broun on Ruth's heroics in the 1923 World Series, from "1923: New York Yankees 4, New York Giants 2" by Broun in the *New York World*, reprinted in *The Baseball Reader* by Charles Einstein

It's as inevitable as tomorrow, but perhaps not as imminent.

—Dodgers executive Branch Rickey on winning it all

It wasn't your basic Picasso.

—Outfielder Rick Monday after a sloppy game in the 1981 World Series

Something odd always happens around him.

—Yankees manager Bob Lemon on his player, Reggie Jackson, after Jackson was involved in a controversial play in the 1978 World Series

Is this really happening? I don't believe what I just saw. One of the most remarkable finishes to any World Series game.

—Announcer Jack Buck on Dodgers star Kirk Gibson's 1988 World Series pinch-homer, from *And the Crowd Goes Wild* by Joe Garner

When the astronauts walked on the moon I figured we had a chance to win. Nothing seemed impossible after that.

—Relief pitcher Tug McGraw on the "Miracle Mets" of 1969

I just wanted to see what happens when one mule confronts three hundred asses.

—A's owner Charlie Finley, explaining why he brought the team mule to the World Series lunch for baseball writers

October. That's when they pay off for playing ball.

—Yankees outfielder Reggie Jackson

The new champions earned what they got and old Alex earned a quiet winter in his rocking chair.

—Writer James R. Harrison on Grover Cleveland Alexander's heroics in the 1926 World Series: "St. Louis Cardinals 3, New York Yankees 2" by Harrison in the *New York Times*, reprinted in *The Baseball Reader* by Charles Einstein

I'm not pressing. I'm just in a slump. I'm too old to be pressing. This is just one of those things. Tomorrow's another day. Got to go day by day, that's all.

—Slugger Tony Perez's take of his 0-for-15 in the 1975 Series

In the back of every player's mind is the hope not to be the goat.

—Orioles infielder Doug DeCinces of World Series play

Let's go on the ball field and hope we all don't get killed.

—Pirates manager Donie Bush sensing impending doom versus the Murderers' Row Yankees before Game One of 1927 World Series

I was trying to will the ball to stay up there and never come down.

—Boston Red Sox catcher Carl Yastrzemski after he had popped out to end the 1978 playoff game versus New York, allowing the Yanks to eventually advance to the World Series

I played here [Cleveland] in the bad years and now to win the pennant. Wow. I'm so thankful to be here and to enjoy it with all of our great fans.

—Indians manager and former player Mike Hargrove, from *The History of the Cleveland Indians* by Richard Rambeck

No sports event in our history has consistently captured the hearts of the public as much as the World Series. Traditionally, it has been the ultimate in sports competition.

—Baseball commissioner Bowie Kuhn

There's no bigger hit than getting the game-winning hit in the World Series. It's a dream. You play that scenario out as a little kid in your backyard or in Little League.

—Arizona's Luis Gonzalez, who drove in the Series-winning run in 2001, from *the Arizona Republic*

We won ballgames we had no business winning. It was kind of magical.

—Pittsburgh pitcher Vernon Law on the Pirates championship season in 1960

Dreams came true in the twelfth—Washington's dream and Walter Johnson's—and when the red September sun dropped down behind the dome of the Capitol the Senators were the baseball champions of the world.

—Sportswriter Bill Corum on the 1924 World Series

I didn't realize it at the time, but after we won the seventh game of the World Series in 1957, everything started to go downhill.

—Hank Aaron of the Braves' fortunes

I know why they threw it at me. What I can't figure out is why they brought it to the ballpark in the first place.

—Cardinals star Joe Medwick after Detroit fans rained down a shower of fruit and garbage on him in the 1934 World Series

They left four days later like Napoleon's troops retreating from Moscow. Napoleon's troops may have left more equipment behind, but George's left more men on base.

—Author Ed Linn on George Steinbrenner's Yankees during the 1981 World Series

It's the first time I ever played on an unnumbered interstate highway.

—Third baseman Graig Nettles of the rock-hard Dodger Stadium infield for the 1978 World Series

The UPS guy made a very nice presentation.

—Catcher Charlie O'Brien, finally receiving his Atlanta World Series ring after moving on to the Blue Jays

How'm I doing, Edna?

—Pitcher Schoolboy Rowe, while being interviewed on the radio during the 1934 Series, addressing his wife; Rowe was later ridiculed by his peers for this comment

If you think it's an advantage, it is. If the other teams think it is, it's a bigger advantage. Actually, it means nothing.

—Pitcher Jerry Reuss on how important experience is during the playoffs

You're shooting for the apex of this game, the World Series. I don't think anything [less] will do for anybody in this clubhouse.

—Atlanta star Chipper Jones, 2001

After seventeen major-league seasons, Roberto Clemente is an overnight sensation.

—Sportswriter Jerry Izenberg on Clemente's surge in fame after his 1971 Series heroics

The million-to-one shot came in. Hell froze over. A month of Sundays hit the calendar. Don Larsen today pitched a no-hit, no-run, no-man-reach-first game in a World Series.

—Sportswriter Shirley Povich on Larsen's 1956 classic

Not playing in a World Series for a great hitter is like not making the Met for a great singer, not playing the Old Vic for a great actor.

—Sportswriter Jim Murray

So far.

—Yankees manager Casey Stengel, responding to a reporter's question if Don Larsen's 1956 Series had been the best game he'd seen Larsen pitch

I know [Sandy] Koufax's weakness. He can't hit.

—Yankees pitcher Whitey Ford, who faced the Dodgers great in the 1963 Series

It was Christmas, the Fourth of July, and Mardi Gras all wrapped into one.

—On the Tigers winning the 1968 World Series, item from the *Detroit Free Press*, no writer listed

It ain't like football. You can't make up no trick plays.

—Manager Yogi Berra on making plans entering the World Series

There isn't a day that I don't think about 1968. Not one single day.

—Tigers star Al Kaline on the lasting impact of winning the World Series, from *USA Today Sports Weekly*

CHAPTER NINE

Wacky Quotes

Some of the quotes from the realm of baseball go beyond merely being funny; they border on the bizarre or the outrageous. In a sport packed with what were once called "flakes," it's only natural that baseball has produced some of the most unnatural quotes in all of sports.

Start with relievers, the facet of baseball so crucial to winning, so pressure filled that one would think all relief pitchers (especially the notoriously zany lefties) must be just one bad outing away from the cardiac unit. Instead, many successful relievers have an equanimity with a devil may care sense of humor to match.

Larry Andersen was a cross between the one-line slinging Henny Youngman and the thought-provoking Steven Wright, and such a blend resulted in some of the wildest and funniest comments in baseball history.

Tug McGraw, father of country singer Tim, had a refreshing, unique take on the game. The southpaw reliever once wrote a fable whose protagonist was a baseball named Larry who had a dream to appear in a World Series. McGraw threw a screwball, at times was accused of being one, and even inspired and worked on a comic strip fittingly entitled "Scroogie."

Others pitchers such as Bill Lee came up with observations that left listeners wondering if Lee was a flake or a philosopher—of course, his nickname, "Spaceman," kind of skewed any such debate.

Like Lee, Jay Hanna Dean's nickname, Dizzy (his brother was Daffy) says it all and, boy, could he come up with some gems. Likewise, Satchel Paige could have authored his own version of Bartlett's book of quotations, baseball style. Like Steve Martin with Dan Aykroyd on the old *Saturday Night Live* skits, ol' Satch was one wild and crazy guy.

Baseball also produced colorful characters Casey Stengel and Yogi Berra, two men widely known for their non sequiturs that left fans laughing while

scratching their heads. Sure, many quotes attributed to them were apocryphal—many, in fact, drummed up by writers—but they're still hilarious.

Toss in Graig Nettles, whose humor ranged from twisted to satiric, and Andy Van Slyke, who could have flourished doing a stand-up act. The list of baseball wits continues unabated and their quotes range from the offbeat to the enigmatic. Enjoy.

You can only be young once, but you can be immature forever.

—Relief pitcher Larry Andersen

Ninety percent I'll spend on good times, women, and Irish whiskey. The other 10 percent I'll probably waste.

—Relief pitcher Tug McGraw

You mean we got to go with people?

—Outfielder Willie Wilson after being told his team was booked on a commercial flight as opposed to a private team flight

I want to thank all of you people for making this night necessary.

—Catcher Yogi Berra

Some day I would like to go up in the stands and boo some fans.

—Pitcher Bo Belinsky

He [manager Charlie Dressen] couldn't fool us. We could hear his footprints.

—Infielder Johnny Logan on Dressen's bed checks

No more than usual.

—First baseman Dick Stuart, when asked if he felt dizzy after being hit by a pitch

Something like four thousand bottles have been thrown at me in my day but only about twenty ever hit me. That does not speak very well for the accuracy of the fans' throwing.

—Umpire Harry "Steamboat" Johnson

I don't need a chest protector. I need a bra.

—Overweight ex-catcher Gus Triandos at an old-timers' game

Most people are dead at my age.

—Manager Casey Stengel, upon turning seventy-five

The Mets have gotten their leadoff batter on base only once in this inning.

—Announcer Ralph Kiner

I was going so bad last week I skipped dinner two days because I was down to 198 [pounds] and I didn't want anyone saying that I wasn't hitting my weight.

—Toronto's Jesse Barfield

In Peck Memorial Hospital.

—Outfielder Pete Reiser, when asked where he believed he'd finish the 1946 season

The way to make coaches think you're in shape in the spring is to get a tan.

—Yankees pitcher Whitey Ford

It's what you dream of right there [a chance to win it in the ninth]—mano a mano, either you're Billy the Kid or Billy the Goat.

—Outfielder Glenn Wilson

This is a tough yard for a hitter when the air conditioning is blowing in.

—Catcher Bob Boone, joking about the Astrodome

You're a liar. There ain't no Hotel Episode in Detroit.

—Zany pitcher Rube Waddell after being fined by his manager for "that disgraceful hotel episode in Detroit"

The only thing running and exercising can do for you is make you healthy.

—Pitcher Mickey Lolich

You know what they [Phillies fans] do when the game is rained out? They go to the airport and boo bad landings.

—Catcher Bob Uecker

Tomorrow is another day. Unless you're not alive.

—White Sox manager Terry Bevington

I don't give a good first impression, or a good second impression. For that matter, I usually come across like a sack of manure.

—Texas manager Doug Rader, soon after being named to that position

He must have made that [movie] before he died.

—Catcher Yogi Berra on actor Steve McQueen

I didn't try too hard. I was afraid I'd get emotionally involved with the cow.

—Infielder Rocky Bridges on his participation in a cow milking contest

They brought me up to the Brooklyn Dodgers, which at that time was in Brooklyn.

—Manager Casey Stengel on his playing days

I ought to get a Black and Decker commercial out of it.

—Pitcher Don Sutton on his alleged scuffing of baseballs

It's all right to have a hitch in your swing but when you have a flaw in your hitch you're in trouble.

—Outfielder Leon Wagner

I have to be careful about eating all the fattening foods they serve. I have to watch my playing weight. But the problem is that I don't know what my playing weight is. I never play.

—Outfielder Joe Lis

The Houston Astrodome is the biggest hairdryer in the world.

—Houston first baseman Joe Pepitone

The highlight of your season is taking the team picture, knowing that the trading deadline has passed and you're a part of the club.

—Ex-catcher Joe Garagiola

Why do people sing "Take Me Out to the Ballgame" when they're already there?

—Relief pitcher Larry Andersen

To a pitcher, a base hit is the perfect example of negative feedback.

—Steve Hovley of the Seattle Pilots

My goals are to hit .300, score 100 runs, and stay injury prone.

—Outfielder Mickey Rivers

Now I won't be able to sign my letters "Senator Henry Bonura, Democrat, Louisiana."

—Zeke Bonura after being swapped from the Senators

Bill Buckner had a nineteen-game hitting streak going and always wore the same underwear. Of course, he didn't have any friends.

—Infielder Lenny Randle

My only regret in life is that I can't sit in the stands and watch me pitch.

—Angels pitcher Bo Belinsky, from *The Suitors of Spring* by Pat Jordan

The wind, the fog rolling in . . . if that's not excitement enough, they ought to just plant land mines arbitrarily in the outfield.

—St. Louis pitcher Joe Magrane on Candlestick Park in San Francisco

Mike Anderson's limitations are limitless.

—Phillies manager Danny Ozark on his outfielder

If people don't want to come to the ballpark, how are you gonna stop them?

—Catcher Yogi Berra

I overslept.

—Outfielder Claudell Washington's explanation for why he was four days late reporting to his new club after being traded

They [kids] should eat the bubble gum, the [baseball trading] cards . . . But bad statistics can't be properly digested, so they should eat the cards of only the good players.

—Third baseman Doug Rader

What the Yankees need is a second-base coach.

—Yankees third baseman Graig Nettles

When he [Darryl] Strawberry punched Keith Hernandez in spring training last season, it was the only time that Strawberry would hit the cutoff man all year.

—Writer Steve Wulf

I don't like tobacco because it causes diseases. Dirt is free and no one bums it off you.

—Mets minor league pitcher Todd Welborn, who chewed dirt instead of tobacco

There's not much to it. You put a right-handed hitter against a left-handed pitcher and a left-handed hitter against a right-handed pitcher, and on cloudy days, you use a fastball pitcher.

—Manager Casey Stengel

What a terrific spitball pitcher he [Bugs Raymond] was. Bugs drank a lot. He didn't spit on the ball. He blew his breath on it and the ball would come up drunk.

—Pitcher Rube Marquard

Some people say you have to be crazy to be a reliever. Well, I don't know, I was crazy before I became one.

—Pitcher Sparky Lyle

I went through life as a "player to be named later."

—Catcher Joe Garagiola

So all those people booing wouldn't know you were my father.

—Sparky Anderson's daughter, Shirlee, after he asked her why she had booed him

What was he doing with Miss Saigon?

—Yankees manager Buck Showalter, when told that the team general manager had gone to see *Miss Saigon* on Broadway

During the years ahead, when you come to a fork in the road, take it.

—Yogi Berra, Yankees catcher

You gotta have a catcher. If you don't have a catcher, you'll have a lot of passed balls.

—Mets skipper Casey Stengel on why he drafted a catcher first in the expansion draft

I'd rather be the Yankees catcher than the president and that makes me pretty lucky, I guess, because I could never be the president.

—Yogi Berra, catcher

They told me to hit. Nobody said anything about running.

—Toronto pitcher Jimmy Key, who seldom went to the plate, after being retired at first on what should have been a hit to the outfield

Even Napoleon had his Watergate.

—Phillies manager Danny Ozark

Does that mean I have to play Hamlet?

—Yankees southpaw Ron Guidry, when told he would fill several roles for the upcoming season

In ten years, Ed Kranepool has a chance to be a star. In ten years, Greg Goossen has a chance to be thirty.

—Mets manager Casey Stengel, when asked about two twenty-year-old prospects on his roster

When he went 0-for-4 he'd wear his uniform in the shower so he could drown the spirits.

—Vic Power on teammate Minnie Minoso, who reportedly believed in voodoo, from *This Side of Cooperstown* by Larry Moffi

"Sorry, Mickey," the Lord said, "but I wanted to give you the word personally. You can't go to heaven because of the way you acted down on earth, but would you mind signing a dozen baseballs?"

—Hall of Famer Mickey Mantle's scenario of his judgment day

I wanted to find out if the diamond was real, so I cut the glass on my coffee table with it. Then I found out the coffee table was worth more than the ring.

—Pitcher Sparky Lyle on his World Series ring

It's youth, but that youth thing gets old after a while.

—Pitching coach Dick Pole on a rookie hurler

I was just in the right place at the right time.

—Reds outfielder Cesar Geronimo on the coincidence of being the three-thousandth strikeout victim of both Nolan Ryan and Bob Gibson

The good Lord was good to me. He gave me a strong body, a good right arm, and a weak mind.

—Pitching great Dizzy Dean

It's like I used to tell my barber. Shave and a haircut, but don't cut my throat, I may want to do that myself.

—Manager Casey Stengel on the frustrations of managing

It's a good thing we won one [game of a doubleheader] or I'd be eating my heart out. As it is, I'm only eating out my right ventricle.

—Outfielder Ron Swoboda

It must be about an elbow specialist.

—Pitcher Steve Stone, when he saw Orioles teammate Jim Palmer reading *Dr. Zhivago*

I don't know. I never smoked Astroturf.

—Reliever Tug McGraw, when asked if he prefers natural grass or Astroturf

There ain't a left-hander in the world that can run a straight line. It's the gravitational pull on the axis of the earth that gets 'em.

—Pitching coach Ray Miller

In Cincinnati, we were lucky to have eyebrows.

—Catcher Dann Bilardello on the Reds policy concerning facial hair

It's déjà vu all over again.

—Catcher Yogi Berra

Let him hit ya'—I'll get you a new neck.

—Casey Stengel, Mets manager, to his player in a bases-loaded situation

Tell Len [Barker] I'm very proud of him. I hope he does better next time.

—Barker's grandmother, Toki Lockhart, upon learning of his perfect game

There's a high chopper over the mound.

—Outfielder Dave Gallagher on seeing a helicopter over the ballpark

I'd walk through hell in a gasoline suit to play baseball.

—Reds legend Pete Rose

Why does sour cream have an expiration date?

—Reliever Larry Andersen

I told you we'd improve our bench.

—Padres manager Jack McKeon upon seeing construction work being done on seats in the dugout

It would take some of the lust off the All-Star Game.

—Hit king Pete Rose on the then new concept of interleague play

Take those players over to that other [spring training] diamond. I want to see if they can play on the road.

—Manager Casey Stengel

I prefer fast food.

—Coach Rocky Bridges on why he doesn't eat snails

That ain't the way to spell my name.

—Catcher Yogi Berra, looking at his check labeled "Pay to Bearer"

Half this game is 90 percent mental.

—Phillies manager Danny Ozark, but also listed as having been said by outfielder Jim Wohlford; also attributed to catcher Yogi Berra as "Baseball is 90 percent mental. The other half is physical." Also by Berra as: "Ninety percent of the game is half mental."

I've seen the future and it's much like the present, only longer.

—Ace Royals reliever Dan Quisenberry

Son, if you want to pitch in the major leagues, you'll have to learn to catch those in your mouth.

—Manager Casey Stengel to a young Yankee who had just committed a balk when a fly buzzed by his eye

I'm not blind to hearing what everybody else hears.

—Pitcher Zane Smith on speculation he would not be kept on Boston's postseason roster

I went to see him about three times and then he went to see a psychiatrist.

—Mitch Williams, lefty pitcher, on visiting a hypnotherapist

I got tired of pulling out my wallet and showing everyone photos.

—Pitcher David Wells on why he decided to get a tattoo of his son on his arm

There's no way they can bury twelve people out there.

—Catcher Bob Kearney of the twelve monuments in centerfield at Yankee Stadium

I'm a household name but not a household word.

—Outfielder Paul Householder

I was so bad, I couldn't have driven Miss Daisy home.

—Pirates outfielder Andy Van Slyke after stranding a slew of teammates

He [Dennis "Oil Can" Boyd] also had a Doberman that acquired a taste for beer. They both cut down, but how would you like to encounter a Doberman kicking a six-pack-a-day beer habit?

—Pitcher Nolan Ryan

How come "fat chance" and "slim chance" mean the same thing?

—Relief pitcher Larry Andersen

If anybody plays harder than Pete Rose, he's gotta be an outpatient.

—Phillies pitcher Tug McGraw

It's not right to throw behind a guy. Every player's got a big behind. Shoot for that instead.

—A's catcher Terry Steinbach

There's no question I'm unpopular and I felt I needed to get away. So I got in my car and pulled up to a Motel 6. They turned the lights off.

—White Sox owner Jerry Reinsdorf

What is a captain supposed to do—go out on the field before the game and decide whether to kick or receive?

—Yankees captain Graig Nettles

I'll take you and a player to be named later.

—6'6" Expos pitcher Dick "The Monster" Radatz to 5'4" Pirate shortstop Fred Patek when a donnybrook broke out

I'm looking forward to putting on my glasses with the fake nose so I can walk around and be a normal person.

—Pitcher Dan Quisenberry on his plans for what to do after the World Series was over

That [the College World Series] was real baseball. We weren't playing for the money. We got Mickey Mouse watches that ran backwards.

—Pitcher Bill Lee

If a horse can't eat it, I don't want to play on it.

—Slugger Dick Allen on artificial turf

He went from Cy Young to sayonara in a year.

—Yankees third baseman Graig Nettles on Sparky Lyle, who won the Cy Young Award in 1977 and then was traded after 1978

My best year was 1965, when I made about $21,000; and $17,000 of that came from selling other players' equipment.

—Bob Uecker, former catcher

I want to pitch my way right into arbitration.

—Twins pitcher Joe Decker's stated goal for the year

I'm not going to wear short pants unless they let me wear a halter top, too.

—Infielder Jack Brohamer, who played for the White Sox when they experimented briefly with the wearing of uniforms which included Bermuda shorts

How can a guy win a game if you don't give him any runs?

—Angels pitcher Bo Belinsky in the seventh inning of a game in which he trailed 15–0.

No, longer than that. Maybe a month and a half.

—Catcher Junior Ortiz, when asked if his injury would keep him on the shelf for six weeks

Those guys [of the Cuban Winter League] couldn't understand the language I was pitching them in. That's why I struck out so many.

—Cardinals pitcher Vinegar Bend Mizell

Does this mean I have to shave my legs?

—Outfielder Andy Van Slyke, when told his team had a policy of no hair below the lip

Thirty-two pounds per square inch at sea level.

—Boston pitcher Bill "Spaceman" Lee when, during the midst of a tight pennant race, he was asked how much pressure he was feeling

Anything that goes that far in the air ought to have a stewardess on it.

—Pitcher Paul Splittorff on a George Brett home run

Sidearm pitchers don't get many breaks from the umpires. They think we are freaks, that we belong on paddy wagons, with lace wrapped around our faces.

—Reliever Dan Quisenberry

The world will end before there's another .400 hitter. I think that was mentioned in the Bible.

—Phillies star Lenny Dykstra

When Charlie Finley had his heart operation, it took eight hours—seven just to find his heart.

—A's pitcher Steve McCatty on his team's owner

I couldn't resist—I had such a great jump on the pitcher.

—Lou Novikoff, outfielder, on stealing third base in a bases-loaded situation

My coordination was so bad I had to pull my car off the side of the road to blow the horn.

—Ellis Clary, infielder

If the Pope was an umpire, he'd still have trouble with the Catholics.

—Umpire Beans Reardon

It was a cross between a screwball and a changeup—a screwup.

—Cubs pitcher Bob Patterson, when asked what pitch he had thrown for a Barry Larkin homer

There's one record I hold: Most World Series on the most different teams for a right-handed third baseman who didn't switch-hit and who never played for the Yankees.

—Heinie Groh, 16-year big-league veteran

We've got a problem. Luis Tiant wants to use the bathroom and it says no foreign objects in the toilet.

—Yankees Graig Nettles, while on a team flight

That's like giving Charles Manson the keys to the city.

—Pitcher Mike Smithson when Dennis "Oil Can" Boyd was presented with a chain saw for doing an interview

Kids should practice autographing baseballs. This is a skill that's often overlooked in Little League.

—Pitcher Tug McGraw

I'd say he's done more than that.

—Manager Yogi Berra, when asked if a player had exceeded his expectations

We used to pray the White Sox and the Cubs would merge so Chicago would have only one bad team.

—Comedian Tom Dreesen, native of Chicago

They [pitchers] shouldn't throw at me—I'm the father of five or six kids.

—Infielder Tito Fuentes

In Boston, as I recall.

—Toronto manager Bobby Mattick, when asked where [what position in the standings] he thought his team would finish the season

You have two hemispheres in your brain—a left and a right side. The left side controls the right side of your body and the right controls the left half. It's a fact. Therefore, left-handed pitchers are the only people in their right minds.

—Southpaw Bill Lee

Things could have easily gone the other way.

—Manager Don Zimmer after completing a road trip his Cubs split, 4–4

Sure I eat what I advertise. Sure I eat Wheaties for breakfast. A good bowl of Wheaties with bourbon can't be beat.

—Pitcher Dizzy Dean

I'm in the twilight of a mediocre career.

—Frank Sullivan, Red Sox pitcher

George is getting to be such a monster that I'd hate to die in a car wreck with the guy. You'd be listed as: Others Killed.

—Royals teammate Clint Hurdle on George Brett's fame

If I ever decide to do a book I've already got the title—*The Bases Were Loaded and So Was I.*

—Infielder Jim Fregosi

The batter still hits a grounder. But in this case the first bounce is 360 feet away.

—Reliever Dan Quisenberry on what happens when his sinkerball isn't working

When I was a kid, I wanted to play baseball and join the circus—with the Yankees, I've been able to do both.

—Graig Nettles of the craziness of the Yankees "Bronx Zoo"

You know Earl [Weaver], he's not happy unless he's not happy.

—Weaver's Baltimore catcher Elrod Hendricks, from *The Umpire Strikes Back* by Ron Luciano

A manager uses a relief pitcher like a six-shooter. He fires until it's empty and then takes the gun and throws it at the villain.

—Reliever Dan Quisenberry

[Lew] Burdette would make coffee nervous.

—Braves manager Fred Haney of his pitcher

They keep me pretty much in the dark about everything. If it [the airplane] had blown up, I wouldn't have known anything about it.

—Pitcher Dennis "Oil Can" Boyd after his team, Boston, didn't inform him about a bomb threat

I'm going to play with harder nonchalance this year.

—Baltimore's Jackie Brandt

Some days you tame the tiger and some days the tiger has you for lunch.

—Pitcher Tug McGraw, also attributed to pitcher Rollie Fingers

I didn't do so hot in the first grade either.

—Pitcher Dizzy Dean on why he quit school after second grade

I wish I could buy you for what you're really worth and sell you for what you think you're worth.

—Yankees great Mickey Mantle to teammate Joe Pepitone

First triple I ever had.

—Pitcher Lefty Gomez of his triple bypass operation

That way I can see where I've been. I always know where I'm going.

—Outfielder Jimmy Piersall on running the bases backward upon hitting his 100th home run

When I was young and smart, I couldn't understand Casey Stengel. Now that I'm older and dumber, he makes sense to me.

—Dodgers great Sandy Koufax

It gets late early out there.

—Hall of Famer Yogi Berra on the difficulty of playing in the shadows of left field in Yankee Stadium

You can't worry if it's cold; you can't worry if it's hot; you only worry if you get sick. Because then if you don't get well, you die.

—Colorful pitcher Joaquin Andujar

A few million years from now the sun will burn out and lose its gravitational pull. The earth will turn into a giant snowball and be hurled through space. When that happens, it won't matter if I get this guy out.

—Pitcher Bill Lee

I will perish this trophy forever.

—Johnny Logan, infielder, upon receiving an award

Fractured, hell. The damn thing's broken.

—Hall of Fame pitcher Dizzy Dean, when told by a doctor that his toe was fractured

All I'm asking for is what I want.

—Stolen base king Rickey Henderson on his money demands during his contract negotiations

Please stop writing those awful stories about me being crazy.

—Outfielder Babe Herman, reportedly said moments before he pulled a lit cigar from his pocket

Once I tried to drown myself with a shower nozzle after I gave up a homer in the ninth. I found out you can't.

—Zany reliever Dan Quisenberry

A lot of relief pitchers develop a crazy facade and it's this facade that helps them deal with the pressure. Of course, maybe it's only the crazies that want to be relief pitchers.

—Reliever Skip Lockwood

If you act like you know what you're doing, you can do anything you want—except maybe perform neural surgery.

—Outfielder John Lowenstein

Most of the time, I don't even know what I said until I read about it. But I really didn't say everything I said.

—Yankees great Yogi Berra

He's missing something upstairs, but that's what makes him a player.

—Utility player Tony Phillips on Angels teammate Rex Hudler

Sometimes I get lazy and let the dishes stack up. But they don't stack too high—I've only got four dishes.

—Flaky Tigers pitcher Mark Fidrych

The more we lose, the more [George] Steinbrenner will fly in and the more he flies, the better the chance there will be a plane crash.

—Yankees star Graig Nettles on the team's controversial owner; also attributed to Dock Ellis by Sparky Lyle in his book *The Bronx Zoo*, coauthored by Peter Golenbock

If I ain't startin', I ain't departin'.

—Shortstop Garry Templeton on his plans for an upcoming All-Star Game

I made a major contribution to the Cardinals' pennant drive in 1964. I got hepatitis.

—Catcher Bob Uecker

How about that tag?

—Third baseman Eddie Mathews as he punched Frank Robinson after Robinson had complained about Mathews having just applied a hard tag on him

A lot of people who don't say "ain't" ain't eating.

—Dizzy Dean, when criticized for using the word *ain't* on the air

That's like throwing Bambi out of the forest.

—Umpire Ron Luciano on being the first ump to toss mild-mannered Mark Belanger from a game, from *The Umpire Strikes Back* by Luciano

There comes a time in every man's life—and I've had plenty of them.

—Colorful manager Casey Stengel

In order to keep doing what we've done, we have to keep doing what we've done in the past.

—Orioles manager Earl Weaver

David Cone is in a class by himself with three or four other players.

—Yankees owner George Steinbrenner

If I knew you was going to pitch a no-hitter, I would have pitched one too.

—Pitcher Dizzy Dean after pitching a three-hitter in the first game of a doubleheader only to see his brother Daffy toss a no-hitter in the nightcap

This [Candlestick Park] wouldn't be such a bad place to play if it wasn't for that wind. I guess that's like saying hell wouldn't be such a bad place if it wasn't so hot.

—Pitcher Jerry Reuss

What can you expect in a 'northpaw' world?

—Lefty reliever Bill Lee, when asked why lefties are such flakes

I can't do that; that's my bad side.

—Catcher Yogi Berra, when told to face the camera directly

How do I know? I haven't caught that pitch yet.

—Catcher Bill DeLancey, answering his manager's question of what the pitch was that had just been ripped for a homer

If I'd known I was gonna pitch a no-hitter today I would have gotten a haircut.

—Pitcher Bo Belinsky

You're the sultan of squat because you spend so much time on the bench.

—Outfielder Merv Rettenmund to backup infielder Larry Brown

Ten-thirty? I'm not even done throwing up at that hour.

—Catcher Jim Pagliaroni

Good pitching will always stop good hitting and vice versa.

—Manager Casey Stengel, also attributed to Bob Veale as: "Good pitching will beat good hitting any time and vice versa."

Sin tax? What will them fellas in Washington think up next?

—Dizzy Dean, upon hearing the word "syntax"

I got good stamina, I got good wind and the heat ain't got me, but I just don't have a good fastball.

—Dodgers pitcher Preacher Roe

If you put his brain in a blue jay, it [the bird] would fly backwards.

—Pitcher Al Nipper on Cubs teammate Mitch Williams

You don't get your first home run too often.

—Catcher Rick Wrona on his first big-league blast

Teaching baseball to five-year-olds is like trying to organize a bunch of earthworms.

—Writer Dorothy C. McConnell

Slump? I ain't in no slump. I just ain't hitting.

—Colorful catcher Yogi Berra

It is beyond my apprehension.

—Danny Ozark, as the Phillies manager

This winter I'm working out every day, throwing at a wall. I'm 11 and 0 against the wall.

—Pitcher Jim Bouton

There is one word in America that says it all and that one word is "You never know."

—Pitcher Joaquin Andujar

What time can you get here?

—St. Louis Browns owner Bill Veeck, straddled with a poor team that wasn't pulling in crowds, to a fan who had called and asked what time that day's game would start

He's the first guy ever to make the major leagues on one brain cell.

—Twins shortstop Roy Smalley on Mickey Hatcher

Instead of looking like an American flag, I look like a taco.

—First baseman Steve Garvey comparing his new Padres uniform with that of his former team, the Dodgers

If horses don't eat it, I don't want to play on it.

—Infielder Dick Allen on artificial turf

There is no homework.

—Pitcher Dan Quisenberry on what he likes best about baseball

Frankly, I'd prefer someplace else.

—Outfielder Babe Herman, responding to an offer to go on an around the world trip

So far I've played right, left, and first base, and I'm Polish. Does that make me a utility pole?

—Frank Kostro, truly a utility player

I'm in the best shape of my life and that includes my brain.

—Phillies outfielder Lenny Dykstra

If he played for me, I wouldn't handle him with a strong arm; I'd handle him with a straightjacket like the rest of the nuts.

—Manager Billy Martin on the flaky Bill Lee

For ten thousand dollars I'd grow one on my butt.

—Pitcher Rollie Fingers after being asked if he, like Joe Namath, would shave his moustache for a TV commercial for a ten-thousand-dollar fee

He'll be okay if he keeps his hand out of his shirt.

—Manager Casey Stengel on Dan Napoleon, outfielder

We [the Phillies] were twenty-four morons and a Mormon.

—Outfielder John Kruk, upon the arrival of Dale Murphy on the team, from *www.webcircle.com*

Remember, half the lies they tell about the Dodgers aren't true.

—Dodgers owner Walter O'Malley

If the Dodgers go to the expense of putting my name on the back of a uniform, I know darn well they aren't going to trade me.

—Infielder Billy Grabarkewitz

It would be an honor to get something like that—I have lots of trophies at home, but I bought them myself.

—Pitcher Bert Blyleven on his thoughts about possibly winning the Comeback Player of the Year award

With the salary I get here, I'm so hollow and starving that I'm liable to explode like a light bulb if I hit the ground too hard.

—Casey Stengel as an outfielder with the Pirates

CHAPTER TEN

The Beauty, Joy, and Love of Baseball

Baseball prose often takes on qualities of poetry. Words flow from pens and off tongues as smoothly and as ornately as icing being squeezed atop a wedding cake.

Many of us who love the game argue that baseball is a sport unlike any other in that it is so powerfully evocative. Gloomy domes and a few other unimaginative cookie-cutter ballparks and bleak facilities such as the Oakland "Mausoleum" aside, even baseball's playing venues have given birth to eternal words of awe; baseball fans and writers alike gush over the beauty of a Camden Yards and a PNC Park of today and display schoolboy nostalgia over the glory of Ebbets and Forbes Fields.

Baseball has spawned volumes of observations which often have good intentions yet are rife with, or border on, mushy sentimentality. Meanwhile, other copious comments on the beauty, joy, and love of the game are downright beautiful in themselves. Both have their place.

Not only that, but those who have penned or spoken those countless words are not just players with a vested interest in the game and members of the media, those assigned to and therefore, obligated to pound out words by the truckload for the companies that purchase ink by the barrel. No, baseball is a topic which has attracted the heavy hitters, the sluggers of the literati, as well. How's this for a roll call: Mark Twain, Robert Frost, James Thurber, Tom Wolfe, William Saroyan, and John Updike, all included in this chapter.

Further, writers in any field don't come much better than, say, Roger Angell, George F. Will, Thomas Boswell, Jim Murray, Red Smith, and Roger Kahn, sportswriters and true devotees of baseball. In the following pages, those who expound on the joy of baseball also include Presidents Franklin D. Roosevelt, Herbert Hoover, and George H. W. Bush.

Plus, it never hurts to take in the words of those who have lived the game, men such as colorful, maverick team owner Bill Veeck, whose love of baseball was deep, and players such as Nolan Ryan and Tom Seaver.

They're all here, professing their love of baseball and marveling at the joy and the beauty of the game.

In the beginning, there was no baseball, but ever since, there have been few beginnings as good as the start of a new baseball season. It's the most splendid time in sport.

—Writer B. J. Phillips

I believe that racial extractions and color hues and forms of worship become secondary to what men can do.

—Baseball executive Branch Rickey

A hot dog at the ballpark is better than steak at the Ritz.

—Actor Humphrey Bogart

You can't sit on a lead and run a few plays into the line and just kill the clock. You've got to throw the ball over the plate and give the other man a chance.

—Orioles manager Earl Weaver

I felt what I almost always feel when I am watching a ballgame: Just for those two or three hours, there is really no place I would rather be.

—Author Roger Angell, from his book *The Summer Game*

I'll be looking at how many years in a row I was able to go out there and be consistent. Not because it was about the dollars or it was about the publicity or whatever, but because the game was meant to be played a certain way.

—Slugger Mo Vaughn on how he'd look back at his career after retiring, from *Baseball Digest*, September 1998

A baseball club is part of the chemistry of the city. A game isn't just an athletic contest. It's a picnic, a kind of town meeting.

—Yankees executive Michael Burke

The best thing about baseball is that you can do something about yesterday tomorrow.

—Manny Trillo, All-Star infielder

Baseball's solitary grace is not obscured in a bedlam of bodies, or in a jarring crash near the goal, or in a madcap scramble near the backboard. Its grace exists to be seen, not clouded . . .

—Author Curt Smith

Nothing flatters me more than to have it assumed that I could write prose—unless it be to have it assumed that I once pitched a baseball with distinction.

—Poet Robert Frost

Baseball is a game of race, creed and color. The race is to first base. The creed is the rules of the game. The color? Well, the home team wears white uniforms and the visiting team wears gray.

—Former catcher Joe Garagiola, from *Baseball Is a Funny Game* by Garagiola

Baseball, so simple, so out-in-the-open, is only brought to its finest stage of appreciation when every detail, every slider low-and-away is studied in the midst of crackling tension.

—Writer Thomas Boswell

Next to religion, baseball has had a greater impact on the American people than any other institution.

—United States president Herbert Hoover

I love the tradition and I love the drama. Every baseball game has drama. It's not just an end-of-the-season thing. I love the pace. I mean, it just works. All the way through.

—Former baseball commissioner Peter Ueberroth

This is a game to be savored, not gulped. There's time to discuss everything between pitches or between innings.

—White Sox owner Bill Veeck, 1981

I never thought about being a writer as I grew up; a writer wasn't something to be. An outfielder was something to be. Most of what I know about style I learned from Roberto Clemente.

—Writer John Sayles

I didn't even graduate from high school. I ate and slept baseball all my life.

—Pitcher Smoky Joe Wood on his love and dedication to the game

I don't think you can think too hard. Baseball, when you really analyze it, is a game within a game within a game.

—Pitcher Skip Lockwood

Baseball is not a life-or-death situation, and in the big picture, this game is just a small part of our lives. The important thing is to use baseball to help other people.

—Superstar Ken Griffey Jr.

Baseball is one of the arts.

—Boston's Ted Williams

Baseball is the working man's game. A baseball crowd is a beer-drinking crowd, not a mixed drink crowd.

—Team owner Bill Veeck

Baseball meant everything to me. If I'd never made the major leagues, I'd probably be playing for some bar for peanuts and cigarettes.

—Hall of Famer Bill Mazeroski, from *More Tales from the Dugout* by Mike Shannon

Baseball is made up of very few big and dramatic moments, but rather it's a beautifully put together pattern of countless little subtleties that finally add up to the big moment, and you have to be well-versed in the game to truly appreciate them.

—Baseball executive Paul Richards

I don't think baseball could survive without all the statistical appurtenances involved in calculating pitching, hitting and fielding percentages. Some people could do without the games as long as they got the box scores.

—Writer John M. Culkin, from the *New York Times*, 1976

You may glory in a team triumphant, but you fall in love with a team in defeat.

—Writer Roger Kahn

Baseball gives every American boy a chance to excel, not just to be as good as someone else but to be better than someone else. That is the nature of man and the name of the game.

—Hall of Famer Ted Williams

Spring is a time of year when the ground thaws, trees bud, the income tax falls due—and everybody wins the pennant.

—Writer Jim Murray

Baseball is not the sport of the wealthy, it is the sport of the wage earner.

—Team owner Bill Veeck

Baseball gives you every chance to be great. Then it puts every pressure on you to prove that you haven't got what it takes. It never takes away the chance and it never eases up on the pressure.

—Joe Garagiola, former big-league catcher

[Winning teams need] a guy who, when the phone rings in the middle of the night, you say, "Oh, no, I hope he's not in trouble."

—Slugger Bobby Bonilla on a feisty sparkplug player like Wally Backman

Give a boy a bat and a ball and a place to play and you'll have a good citizen.

—Hall of Famer Joe McCarthy

I always wonder if the fans are seeing enough. If you stay with this game and really watch it, your appreciation goes much deeper. It rewards you.

—Hall of Fame catcher Ted Simmons

If you see a wrong and make an effort to correct it, you shouldn't seek recognition for doing so.

—Executive Branch Rickey, referring to signing baseball's first African-American player, Jackie Robinson

I don't think about a big home run or a big play in the field. I think about warming up in left field and looking out behind the stadium and seeing thousands of people rushing into the ballpark for the first pitch.

—Outfielder Art Shamsky

Baseball is the most unchanging thing in our society—an island of stability in an unstable world, an island of sanity in an insane world.

—Team owner Bill Veeck

Good players feel the kind of love for the game that they did when they were Little Leaguers.

—Hall of Fame pitcher Tom Seaver

Every player should be accorded the privilege of at least one season with the Chicago Cubs. That's baseball as it should be played—in God's own sunshine. And that's really living.

—Cubs infielder Alvin Dark

The crowd as a whole plays the role of Greek chorus to the actors on the field below. It reflects every action, every movement, every changing phase of the game. It keens. It rejoices, it moans.

—Author Paul Gallico

You should enter a ballpark the way you enter a church.

—Pitcher Bill Lee

The clock doesn't matter in baseball. Time stands still or moves backward. Theoretically, one game could go on forever.

—Herb Caen, writer for *the San Francisco Chronicle*

Baseball is not precisely a team sport. It is more a series of concerts by artists.

—Writer Jim Murray

Baseball is the very symbol, the outward and visible expression of the drive and push and rush and struggle of the raging, tearing, booming nineteenth century.

—Author Mark Twain

[Baseball] is also an important social institution in our complex American society. Recognized as the "national game," it has become a symbol of America in much the same way that the Olympic Games are associated with Greece or cricket with England.

—Harold Seymour, PhD, author, former big league scout, from the *New-York Historical Society Quarterly*, 1956, reprinted in *The Complete Armchair Book of Baseball*, edited by John Thorn

When a poor American boy dreamed of escaping his grim life, his fantasy probably involved becoming a professional baseball player. It was not so much the national sport as the binding national myth.

—Writer David Halberstam

I can never understand why anybody leaves the game early to beat the traffic. The purpose of baseball is to keep you from caring if you beat traffic.

—Columnist Bill Vaughan

Baseball is the fabric of the American soul. The cliché goes: Baseball is as American as apple pie. I say more so. You can buy apple pie anywhere, but baseball is still a kid and his father shagging fly balls on a June afternoon at the park.

—Larry King, television host, from *What Baseball Means to Me*, edited by Curt Smith

Baseball is the only game left for people. To play basketball now, you have to be 7'6". To play football you have to be the same width.

—Team owner Bill Veeck

Baseball fans love numbers. They like to swirl them around their mouths like Bordeaux wine.

—Author Pat Conroy

You can go to the ballpark on a quiet Tuesday afternoon with only a few thousand people in the place and thoroughly enjoy a one-sided game. Baseball has an esthetic, intellectual appeal found in no other sport.

—Baseball commissioner Bowie Kuhn

Whoever would understand the heart and mind of America had better learn baseball.

—Writer Jacques Barzun in *God's Country and Mine*, from *The Baseball Reader* by Charles Einstein

If you're not having fun in baseball, you miss the point of everything.

—First baseman Chris Chambliss

One of the beautiful things about baseball is that every once in a while you come into a situation where you want to, and where you have to, reach down and prove something.

—Pitching great Nolan Ryan

The only guys I care about are the other twenty-four guys on my team.

—Slugger Ken Griffey Jr. on the importance of team unity

Two events are supremely beautiful: the strikeout and the home run. Each is a difficult and unlikely thing flawlessly achieved before your eyes.

—Author and playwright William Saroyan

There are three things in my life which I really love. God, my family, and baseball. The only problem—once baseball season starts, I change the order around a bit.

—Infielder Al Gallagher

Baseball is a ballet without music. Drama without words. A carnival without kewpie dolls. Baseball is continuity. Pitch to pitch. Inning to inning. Season to season.

—Tigers broadcaster Ernie Harwell from *Baseball and the Meaning of Life*, edited by Josh Leventhal

Baseball is a sport dominated by vital ghosts; it's a fraternity, like no other we have, of the active and the no longer so, the living and the dead.

—Writer Richard Gilman

I felt like my bubble gum card collection had come to life.

—Actor James Garner at an awards dinner he attended with many baseball stars, c.1968

For the rest of my life, I'll look at the back of that bubble gum card and I'll see that year.

—Angels star Darin Erstad on his great 2000 season

Major league baseball has done as much as any one thing in this country to keep up the spirits of the people.

—United States president Franklin D. Roosevelt

Football is to baseball as blackjack is to bridge. One is the quick jolt; the other the deliberate, slow-paced game of skill.

—Dodger broadcaster Vin Scully

The majority of American males put themselves to sleep by striking out the batting order of the New York Yankees.

—Author James Thurber

I believe in the Rip Van Winkle theory—that a man from 1910 must be able to wake up after being asleep for 70 years, walk into a ballpark, and understand baseball perfectly.

—Bowie Kuhn, commissioner of baseball

Baseball has been the most exciting and frustrating experience of my life. In movies, I never lost a fight. In baseball, I hardly ever won one.

—Angels owner and former film star Gene Autry, from *The Anaheim Angels* by Ross Newhan

I think there are only three things America will be known for two thousand years from now when they study this civilization: the Constitution, jazz music, and baseball.

—Writer Gerald Early

Say this much for big league baseball, it is beyond any question the greatest conversation piece ever invented in America.

—Writer/historian Bruce Catton

Any baseball is beautiful. No other small package comes as close to the ideal in design and utility. It is a perfect object for a man's hand. Pick it up and it instantly suggests its purpose: It is meant to be thrown a considerable distance—thrown hard and with precision.

—Sportswriter Roger Angell, from *Five Seasons*

Other sports are just sports; baseball is a love.

—Television personality Bryant Gumbel

Baseball? It's just a game—as simple as a ball and a bat. Yet, as complex as the American spirit it symbolizes. It's a sport, business—and sometimes even religion.

—Hall of Fame announcer Ernie Harwell, from *Tuned to Baseball*

Baseball is as much a part of America as the freedoms we cherish and the liberties we defend.

—Reds general manager Bob Howsam

No game in the world is as tidy and dramatically neat as baseball with cause and effect, crime and punishment, motive and result so cleanly defined.

—Sportswriter Paul Gallico

Baseball is almost the only orderly thing in a very unorderly world. If you get three strikes, even the best lawyer in the world can't get you off.

—Team owner Bill Veeck

It also makes it easy for the generations to talk to one another.

—Poet Joel Oppenheimer on the joys of baseball

Baseball is green and safe. It has neither the street intimidation of basketball nor the controlled Armageddon of football. . . . Baseball is a green dream that happens on summer nights in safe places in unsafe cities.

—Author Luke Salisbury

To walk out and feel your spikes in the grass is a good feeling.

—Outfielder Reggie Jackson

It's not just a ballgame, you bum, it's art, religion.

—Writer Dan Shaughnessy

You can't freeze the ball in this game. You have to play till the last man is out.

—Hall of Fame manager Joe McCarthy

Baseball was an experience you couldn't buy for money. Once you get established as a regular, you couldn't buy that. There's no way in the world I could explain it to you. It teaches you so much and broadens your mind. It makes you feel like you are somebody.

—Pitcher Guy Bush

Baseball happens to be a game of cumulative tension. . . . Football, basketball, and hockey are played with hand grenades and machine guns.

—Writer John Leonard

I see great things in baseball. It is our game. The American game. It will repair our losses and be a blessing to us.

—Walt Whitman, poet

Baseball put me in multiracial situations at a very early age. It was there that I realized that we will not fulfill our ideals until we can see deeper than skin color to the individual.

—NBA star and US Senator Bill Bradley, from *What Baseball Means to Me*, edited by Curt Smith

Ballparks should be happy places. They should always smell like freshly cut grass.

—Team owner Bill Veeck

The umpires always say, “Play ball.” They don’t say “Work ball.”

—Hall of Famer Willie Stargell

Any minute, any day, some players may break a long-standing record. That’s one of the fascinations about the game—the unexpected surprises.

—Manager and team owner Connie Mack

I like to look down on a field of green and white, a summertime land of Oz, a place of dream. I’ve never been unhappy in a ballpark.

—Writer Jim Murray

Baseball can survive anything.

—Bill Terry, as the manager of the New York Giants

You have to grow up playing it. You have to accept the lore of the bubble gum card and believe that if the answer to the Mays-Mantle-Snider question is found, then the universe will be a simpler and more ordered place.

—Writer David Halberstam

I firmly believe if you want a boy to grow up and be a success in any line, you should teach him baseball, to have him understand it and play it.

—Former Florida governor Leroy Collins

Only boring people find baseball boring.

—Sportswriter Peter Golenbock

Baseball has done more to move America in the right direction than all the professional patriots with all their cheap words.

—Giants outfielder Monte Irvin

That's the true harbinger of spring, not crocuses or swallows returning to Capistrano, but the sound of a bat on the ball.

—Team owner Bill Veeck

Baseball has a cleanness. If you do a good job, the numbers say so. You don't have to ask anyone or play politics. You don't have to wait for reviews.

—Dodgers great Sandy Koufax from *Baseball and the Meaning of Life,* edited by Josh Leventhal

I wish people would watch baseball the way ballet fans watch the dance—not to see who wins but to see how well each player performs his art.

—Relief pitcher and Cy Young Award–winner Mike Marshall

Only in baseball can a team player be a pure individualist first and a team player second, within the rules and the spirit of the game.

—Executive Branch Rickey

Fenway Park, in Boston, is a lyric little bandbox of a ball park. Everything is painted green and seems in curiously sharp focus, like the inside of an old-fashioned peeping-type Easter egg.

—Writer John Updike

In a confused and confusing world in which the underpinnings are less stable than the shifting sand, more like a quagmire, baseball is an island of stability.

—Bill Veeck, author and team owner

The meat-and-potatoes sport—baseball.

—Newspaper writer Red Smith

It is designed to break your heart. The game begins in the spring, when everything else begins again, and it blossoms in the summer, filling the afternoons and evenings, and then as soon as the chill rains come, it stops and leaves you to face the fall alone.

—A. Bartlett Giamatti, Commissioner of Baseball

The beauty and joy of baseball is not having to explain it.

—Cubs team publicist Chuck Shriver

Is there anything that can evoke spring—the first, fine days of April—better than the sound of the ball smacking into the pocket of the big mitt, the sound of the bat as it hits the horse hide?

—Author Thomas Wolfe

I venture to say that there are millions of adults who would give almost anything to have been a major league ballplayer for just a day.

—Manager Charlie Grimm

Baseball is the most intellectual game because most of the action goes on in your head.

—Former United States Secretary of State Henry Kissinger

Hope rises each spring like sap in the trees. That's part of baseball, that's one of the greatest things about the game. You have the annual rebirth no matter how disastrous the previous year was.

—Brewers general manager Harry Dalton

What baseball means to me . . . A sense of continuity . . . A cavalcade of characters . . . Enough anecdotes to fill a hundred rain delays . . . Debates that always rage and are almost never settled . . . Familiar surroundings, always holding the possibility of something you'd never expect.

—From *What Baseball Means to Me*, edited by Curt Smith

It is played by people, real people, not freaks. Basketball is played by giants. Football is played by corn-fed hulks. The normal-sized man plays baseball and the fellow in the stands can relate to that.

—Team owner Bill Veeck

There is nothing in life as constant and as changing at the same time as an afternoon at a ballpark.

—Televison host Larry King

On any given day . . . come out to the ballpark and you'll see something different.

—Sportswriter Fred Borsch

It doesn't take much to get me up for baseball. Once the national anthem plays, I get chills.

—Batting champ Pete Rose

Every day is a new opportunity. You can build on yesterday's success or put its failures behind and start over again. That's the way life is, with a new game every day, and that's the way baseball is.

—Hall of Famer Bob Feller, from *Baseball and the Meaning of Life*, edited by Josh Leventhal

Baseball, it is said, is only a game. True, and the Grand Canyon is only a hole in Arizona. Not all holes, or games, are created equal.

—Writer George F. Will

The great American game should be an unrelenting war of nerves.

—Tiger great Ty Cobb

Never let the odds keep you from pursuing what you know in your heart you were meant to do.

—Satchel Paige, Hall of Fame pitcher

Sometimes I'd go into Dodger Stadium just to be alone. The game might start at eight and I'd get there at one and sit in the stands and look at the field. It was beautiful.

—Dodgers infielder Jim Lefebvre

Man may penetrate the outer reaches of the universe. He may solve the very secret of eternity itself. But for me the ultimate human experience is to witness the flawless execution of the hit and run.

—Baseball executive Branch Rickey

The whole history of baseball has the quality of mythology.

—Author Bernard Malamud

For many, baseball cards are the last toy as well as the first possession. You fall in love with them as a child, then leave them behind at puberty. They line the blue-water, lazy-day joy of childhood summers with the pride of blossoming maturity.

—Writer Thomas Boswell

The origins of modern baseball are shrouded in history, but it is a well-established fact that baseball was the first professional sport to appeal to the masses.

—Writer George H. Sage

Kids are always chasing rainbows, but baseball is a world where you can catch them.

—Pitcher Johnny Vander Meer

Almost the only place in life where a sacrifice is really appreciated.

—The definition of baseball from Mark Beltaire, *Webster's New World Dictionary of Quotable Definitions*

It is said that you never forget your first love. For me, that is Barbara. But a runner-up is baseball.

—George H. W. Bush, former president of the United States, from *What Baseball Means to Me*, edited by Curt Smith

To compare baseball with other team games is to say the Hope Diamond is a nice chunk of carbon. The endless variety of physical and mental skills demanded by baseball is both uncomparable and incomparable.

—Bill Veeck, team owner

A baseball fan has the digestive appetite of a billy goat. He can and does devour any set of diamond statistics with an insatiable appetite and then nuzzles hungrily for more.

—Sportswriter Arthur Daley

Baseball gives . . . a growing boy self-poise and self-reliance. Baseball is a man maker.

—Baseball pioneer and Hall of Famer Albert Spalding

At the beginning of the World Series of 1947, I experienced a completely new emotion when the National Anthem was played. This time, I thought, it is being played for me, as much as for anyone else.

—Dodgers star Jackie Robinson, who broke the "color line" in baseball that season

I don't care how long you've been around, you'll never see it all.

—Bob Lemon, as the White Sox manager

Baseball is more than a game to me—it's a religion.

—Umpire Bill Klem

In winter, I get cabin fever bad. I wish I had a tape recording of the sounds of batting practice.

—Pitching coach Ray Miller

Wrigley Field is a Peter Pan of a ballpark. It has never grown up and it has never grown old.

—Sportswriter E. M. Swift

It [baseball] combines in perfect harmony the magnificent features of ballet, drama, art, and ingenuity.

—Commissioner Bowie Kuhn

What's important is that baseball, after 28 years of artificial turf and expansion and the designated hitter and drugs and free agency and thousand dollar bubblegum cards, is still a gift given by fathers to sons.

—Writer Michael Chabon, from the *New York Times Magazine*, 1991

It was everything and more. Those nine years of bus rides, bad food, bad hotels, bad fans—it was all worth it.

—Pete Rose Jr. after playing in his first big league game, from *Tales from the Ballpark* by Mike Shannon

I love going to spring training because it seems like baseball in its purest sense, the same game we played as kids. The scores don't mean anything; no one cares about the standings. It's just the game that matters.

—Sports talk show host Pete Franklin

What's important is that kids discover that baseball is fun and that it gets to be more fun as you get better at it.

—Yankees great Mickey Mantle

Baseball, to me, is still the national pastime, because it is a summer game. I feel that almost all Americans are summer people, that summer is what they think of when they think of their childhood.

—Pitcher Steve Busby

THOSE QUOTED

A

Aaron, Hank: outfielder, Hall of Famer, hit 755 lifetime homers, no man has ever driven in as many runs as Aaron.

Aaron, Herbert: Hank's father

Alexander, Grover Cleveland: Hall of Fame pitcher, won 373 games, posting a .642 WL%

Allen, Bob: Braves publicity director

Allen, Dick: All-Star slugger, drove in 1,119 runs, won an MVP Award

Allen, Ethan: outfielder for 1,123 games, once led his league in doubles

Alomar, Robbie: 10-time Gold Glove winner and All-Star, 1990 to 2001

Alomar, Sandy Jr.: All-Star catcher, won the 1990 Rookie of the Year Award and appeared in two World Series

Alston, Walt: World Series–winning manager, won 2,040 games

Andersen, Larry: zany/clever pitcher, 17-year veteran who appeared in the 1983 and 1993 World Series

Anderson, Shirlee: daughter of Sparky

Anderson, Sparky: entered Hall of Fame in 2000, won World Series with both the Reds and Tigers

Andujar, Joaquin: former big-league pitcher, All-Star who twice won 20 contests

Angell, Roger: author

Appling, Luke: major league shortstop and member of the Hall of Fame

Ashburn, Richie: Hall of Fame outfielder and announcer, hit .308 lifetime

Asinof, Elliot: author

Aspromonte, Bob: third baseman from 1956 through 1971

Aspromonte, Ken: managed the Cleveland Indians for three seasons, played seven seasons in the majors as an infielder

Auker, Elden: known as "Submarine," he was a 10-year veteran pitcher

Autry, Gene: singer, movie star, and former owner of the Angels

Averill, Earl: Hall of Fame outfielder of 13 seasons, led his league once in triples

B

Baer, Arthur: sportswriter

Bailey, Ed: major league catcher and five-time All-Star

Bamberger, George: big-league manager, winner of 458 games

Banks, Ernie: member of the 500 home run club, Hall of Famer, shortstop/first baseman

THOSE QUOTED

Bannister, Alan: veteran infielder

Barfield, Jesse: Gold Glove winning outfielder and All-Star, hit 241 career homers

Barfield, Josh: infielder, broke in with the Padres in 2006

Barney, Rex: former pitcher for Brooklyn and announcer

Barrett, Red: major league pitcher between 1937 and 1949, All-Star in 1945

Barry, Dave: humorist

Barzun, Jacques: writer

Baylor, Don: manager and All-Star veteran of 19 seasons, owns 1,276 RBIs

Beane, Billy: baseball general manager, played 118 big-league games

Beard, Gordon: sportswriter

Belanger, Mark: slick fielding shortstop who won eight Gold Gloves and appeared in four World Series

Belcher, Tim: 14-year veteran pitcher and winner of 146 games

Bell, Buddy: major league third baseman, All-Star, later a coach and manager

Bell, Cool Papa: inducted into the Hall of Fame as a Negro Leagues player, reputedly one of the fastest players ever

Bell, Les: nine-year veteran third baseman

Belle, Albert: outfielder/designated hitter who hit 381 homers over 12 seasons

Belinsky, Bo: colorful major league pitcher yet won only 28 games over eight seasons

Beltaire, Mark: newspaper columnist

Bench, Johnny: major league catcher and Hall of Famer, once held record for the most career homers by a catcher

Bender, Chief: 212-game winner, primarily with the Philadelphia A's, led AL in WL% once, Hall of Famer

Benedict, Bruce: All-Star catcher, spent 12 seasons with Atlanta

Bengough, Benny: big-league catcher for 10 seasons

Benzinger, Todd: played nine seasons, mostly in the outfield, led the NL in at-bats in 1989

Berg, Moe: former big-league catcher of 15 seasons, was a multi-linguist

Berra, Yogi: Hall of Fame catcher, still holds record for most hits in World Series play, 71

Bevington, Terry: managed three seasons for the White Sox

Bilardello, Dann: catcher for eight seasons between 1983 and 1992

Billingham, Jack: winner of 145 games, was on World Series-winning Reds team in 1975 and '76

Bisher, Furman: sportswriter

Blass, Steve: ex-pitcher and broadcaster

Blefary, Curt: played eight seasons, mainly in the outfield, and appeared in the 1966 World Series

Blue, Vida: winner of 209 big league games, won the AL Cy Young Award and MVP in 1971

Bluege, Ossie: Washington Senators third baseman of 18 seasons, and All-Star in 1935

Blyleven, Bert: pitched 22 years, won 287 games, and possessed one of the greatest curveballs ever

Boddicker, Mike: 14-season veteran pitcher and MVP of the 1983 ALCS

Bogart, Humphrey: actor

Boggs, Tommy: pitcher for nine seasons

Boggs, Wade: member of the Hall of Fame, third baseman who led the AL in hitting five times, and amassed 3,010 hits

Bonds, Barry: number one on the all-time home run list with 762

Bonilla, Bobby: veteran of 16 seasons, once drove in 120 runs, six-time All-Star

Bonura, Zeke: first baseman for seven seasons, hit a high of 27 home runs as a rookie in 1934

Boone, Bob: All-Star catcher, won seven Gold Gloves, banged out 1,838 lifetime hits

Borsch, Fred: sportswriter

Boswell, Thomas: author

Boudreau, Lou: Hall of Fame shortstop and manager, 1948 AL MVP

Bouton, Jim: major league pitcher and author

Bowa, Larry: two-time Gold Glove winner at shortstop and five-time All-Star

Boyd, Dennis: nicknamed "Oil Can," pitched for 10 seasons, primarily with Boston, and won 78 big-league games

Boyer, Clete: 16-year veteran third baseman, Gold Glove winner

Bradley, Bill: former NBA star and US Senator

Bragan, Bobby: former infielder/catcher and big-league manager

Branca, Ralph: pitched a dozen seasons primarily for Brooklyn, a three-time All-Star

Brandt, Jackie: played outfielder for 11 seasons, winning Gold Glove in 1959

Brett, George: Kansas City Royals star and Hall of Famer, member of 3,000-hit club

Brewer, Chet: Negro Leagues pitcher

Bricker, Charles: sportswriter

Bridges, Rocky: colorful infielder and manager, hit .247 over 11 big-league seasons

Bristol, Dave: former big-league manager who won 657 games

Brock, Lou: Hall of Fame outfielder, former record holder for most steals in a season (118)

Brohamer, Jack: infielder who played nine seasons, mainly for the Indians

Brosius, Scott: All-Star third baseman of 11 seasons, his career high was .304 in 1996

Brosnan, Jim: major league pitcher and author

Broun, Heywood: sportswriter

Brown, Bobby: New York Yankee of eight seasons, primarily third baseman, who later became a doctor and AL president

Brown, Gates: outfielder of 13 seasons, hit 84 career homers, was on 1968 champion Tigers

Brown, Kevin: All-Star pitcher who won a career-high 21 games in 1992

Brown, Warren: sportswriter

Brye, Steve: nine-year veteran outfielder

Buck, Jack: Hall of Fame announcer

Buckner, Bill: played 22 seasons hitting .289 lifetime, led the NL in hitting in 1980

Buhl, Bob: major league pitcher

Bunning, Jim: Hall of Fame pitcher and winner of 224 games over 17 seasons

Burdette, Lew: won 203 games and was a two-time All-Star, also won three games in the 1957 World Series

Burke, Michael: New York Yankees executive

Burkett, John: All-Star pitcher, 15-year veteran, won 166 games

Burns, Britt: Chicago White Sox pitcher, 70–60 W-L record

Busby, Steve: pitched eight seasons with two no-hitters to his credit

Bush, Donie: shortstop for 16 seasons, mainly with the Tigers, led the AL in runs scored in 1917, later became a manager

Bush, George H. W.: former president of the US

Bush, Guy: pitcher for 17 seasons and winner of 176 big-league games, pitched in two World Series

C

Cabell, Enos: played 15 seasons, hit a career-high .311 in 1983

Caen, Herb: sports columnist

Campanella, Roy: Hall of Fame catcher, appeared in five World Series, was a three-time MVP

Candiotti, Tom: knuckleball pitcher for 16 seasons, winner of 151 games

Cannon, Jimmy: sportswriter

Canseco, Jose: All-Star outfielder/designated hitter, appeared in four World Series, won the Rookie of the Year Award and an MVP

Caray, Harry: Hall of Fame announcer

Caray, Skip: Atlanta Braves announcer

Carew, Rod: Hall of Fame infielder who compiled 3,053 hits, famous for great bat control

Carroll, Clay: 15-year relief pitcher with 143 saves

Carson, Johnny: TV celebrity, host of *The Tonight Show*

Carty, Rico: outfielder/designated hitter for 15 seasons, hit .366 in 1970, tops in the NL

Cash, Norm: Detroit Tigers star first baseman, won batting crown in 1961

Cashen, Frank: baseball executive

Cepeda, Orlando: nicknamed the "Baby Bull," played 17 seasons, mainly at first base, and entered the Hall of Fame in 1999

Chandler, Happy: former baseball commissioner

Chavez, Endy: through 2006 has played six years, hit a high of .306 in 2006

Chabon, Michael: writer

Chambliss, Chris: 1971 AL Rookie of the Year, All-Star first baseman, hit 185 lifetime home runs

Chylak, Nestor: major league umpire

Clark, Jack: outfielder/first baseman, four-time All-Star, hit a career-high .306 in 1978

Clary, Ellis: major league scout and former infielder

Clemente, Roberto: Hall of Fame outfielder, racked up 3,000 lifetime hits and won 12 Gold Glove Awards

Clemens, Roger: Pitched for 24 seasons, winning 354 games, while winning seven Cy Young Awards, also led his league in ERA seven times

Clines, Gene: outfielder, hit a career-high .334 in 1972

Clyde, David: major league pitcher who debuted in the bigs right out of high school

Cobb, Ty: former all-time hit king, Hall of Famer, ranks number one for lifetime batting average

Cochrane, Mickey: Hall of Fame catcher who won two MVP Awards and was a .320 lifetime hitter

Cohn, Lowell: sportswriter

Colavito, Rocky: major league outfielder known for his rifle arm and power hitting

Colborn, Jim: pitched 10 seasons, he was a 20-game winner in 1973

Collins, Dave: outfielder for 16 seasons, led AL in triples in 1984

Collins, Eddie: Hall of Fame second baseman and member of the 3,000-hit club

Collins, Leroy: former governor of Florida

Comiskey, Charles A.: owner of the Chicago White Sox

Cone, David: All-Star pitcher, winner of 194 games and 1994 Cy Young Award winner

Conlan, Jocko: former major league umpire

Conley, Gene: veteran pitcher of 11 seasons and a three-time All-Star

Conroy, Pat: author

Cook, Dennis: 15-year veteran pitcher who appeared in 665 games

Corrales, Pat: former catcher, coach, and manager

Corum, Bill: sportswriter

Cosell, Howard: announcer

Costas, Bob: sportscaster

Coveleski, Stan: Hall of Fame pitcher who won 215 games and appeared in two World Series

Cox, Bobby: Hall of Fame manager who won 2,504 games

Craig, Roger: big-league manager and coach, early proponent of the splitter, former pitcher

Crandall, Del: former All-Star catcher and big-league manager

Crawford, Sam: Hall of Fame outfielder, ranks first for career triples with 309

Cronin, Joe: Hall of Fame shortstop and manager, lead AL in doubles twice

Cummings, Candy: Hall of Fame pitcher credited with the discovery of the curveball

Curtis, John: major league pitcher for 15 seasons, once won 13 games

D

Daley, Arthur: sportswriter

Dalton, Harry: former baseball general manager

Daly, Dan: author

Damon, Johnny: In 18 major league seasons, the outfielder had a .284 lifetime average, was a two-time All-Star, part of the Red Sox world championship in 2004

Dark, Alvin: infielder and manager, hit .289 lifetime

Darling, Ron: an All-Star pitcher in 1985, appeared in 1986 World Series, and won 136 games lifetime

Davidson, Donald: major league traveling secretary

Dawson, Andre: All-Star outfielder, endured for 21 seasons, hit 438 homers

Dean, Dizzy: Hall of Fame pitcher, later became a colorful announcer, was a 30-game winner

DeCinces, Doug: All-Star third baseman of 15 seasons and Silver Slugger Award winner in 1982

Decker, Joe: played nine seasons between 1969 and 1979, winning 36 games lifetime

Delgado, Carlos: All-Star first baseman in 2000 and 2003, winner of the 2000 AL Hank Aaron Award

DeLancey, Bill: caught 180 games over four seasons for the Cardinals

DeMars, Billy: longtime coach and former shortstop

Dickey, Bill: Hall of Fame Yankees catcher, lifetime .313 hitter, appeared in eight World Series

Dierker, Larry: pitcher, announcer, and manager, two-time All-Star who once won 20 games

DiMaggio, Joe: Yankees superstar and Hall of Famer, owns a .325 lifetime batting average

DiSarcina, Gary: shortstop for 12 seasons, All-Star in 1995

Donnelly, Rich: major league coach

Downing, Al: appeared in three World Series, famous for surrendering Hank Aaron's record-breaking 715th home run

Dreesen, Tom: comedian

Dressen, Charlie: major league manager

Dryden, Charles: sportswriter

Drysdale, Don: Hall of Fame pitcher, winner of 209 games

Durocher, Leo: major league infielder and manager, posthumously inducted into Hall of Fame

Dykes, Jimmy: All-Star infielder and manager (was a player/manager for six years)

Dykstra, Lenny: outfielder for 12 seasons, a member of two World Series squads

E

Early, Gerald: writer

Eckersley, Dennis: Hall of Fame pitcher, member of the World Series-winning A's of 1989, saved 390 games

Edmonds, Jim: All-Star outfielder played 14 seasons and won eight Gold Glove Awards

Edwards, Doc: former big-league manager for three seasons, former catcher

Erskine, Carl: All-Star Dodgers pitcher, won 122 in 12 years, had a .610 WL% lifetime

Erstad, Darin: first baseman/outfielder who played 11 seasons and won three Gold Gloves

Espinosa, Nino: eight-year veteran pitcher, won 44 games lifetime

Estrada, Chuck: former pitcher and pitching coach

Evans, Dwight: 20-year vet, owns eight Gold Glove Awards, was in three All-Star Games

F

Face, Roy: pitched 16 seasons, enjoyed a 18–1 season in 1959

Feller, Bob: Hall of Fame pitcher, strikeout king, and winner of 266 games

Fidrych, Mark: "the Bird," two-time All-Star who went 19–9 as a rookie for the Tigers in 1976

Fimrite, Ron: sportswriter

Fingers, Rollie: Hall of Fame reliever who recorded 341 career saves, seven-time All-Star

Finley, Charlie: former owner of the Oakland A's

Fischer, Bill: coach and major league pitcher for nine seasons

Fisk, Carlton: Hall of Fame catcher, Rookie of the Year Award winner, 376 career homers

Flanagan, Mike: Cy Young Award–winning pitcher for the Orioles

Flood, Curt: major league outfielder, contested baseball's reserve clause, and was an All-Star outfielder

Floyd, Cliff: played in the 1997 World Series for Florida and hit 233 homers in 17 big-league seasons

Ford, Whitey: New York Yankees pitcher and member of the Hall of Fame, won 236 games

Foster, George: played 18 seasons and drove 1,239 runs, five-time All-Star outfielder

Fowler, Art: nine-year veteran pitcher and highly-regarded coach

Foxx, Jimmie: hit 534 career homers, Hall of Fame first baseman

Frank, Stanley: sportswriter

Franklin, Pete: sports talk show host

Franks, Herman: major league manager and former catcher

Frazier, George: relief pitcher of 10 seasons, appeared in two World Series

Frederick, Johnny: outfielder, played six seasons for Brooklyn, hit a career-high 24 home runs as a rookie

Fregosi, Jim: former infielder and manager, hit .265 lifetime

Frey, Jim: manager for the Royals and Cubs

Frick, Ford: former baseball commissioner

Frisch, Frankie: Hall of Famer, infielder and manager, owned 2,880 career hits

Frost, Robert: poet

Fryman, Travis: All-Star third baseman, drove in a career high 106 runs in 2000

Fuentes, Tito: second baseman for 13 seasons, mainly with the Giants

Funk, Frank: baseball coach

G

Gale, Rich: pitched seven seasons, winning a career-high 14 as a rookie in 1978

Gallagher, Al: third baseman for four seasons, 1970 through 1973

Gallagher, Dave: outfielder for nine seasons, a .271 lifetime hitter

Gallico, Paul: author, sportswriter

Gamble, Oscar: outfielder/designated hitter who appeared in 1,584 games over 17 seasons

Garagiola, Joe: major league catcher and colorful broadcaster

Gardner, Billy: major league infielder and manager

Garner, James: actor

Garvey, Steve: All-Star first baseman who hit 272 lifetime homers over 19 seasons

Gehrig, Lou: Hall of Fame first baseman

Gehringer, Charlie: a.k.a. "the Mechanical Man," he hit .320 lifetime, member of Hall of Fame

Geronimo, Cesar: played 15 seasons, was a part of the "Big Red Machine," and won four Gold Gloves

Giamatti, A. Bartlett: commissioner of baseball

Giambi, Jason: All-Star first baseman/designated hitter, 2000 MVP winner

Gibson, Bob: Hall of Fame pitcher and winner of 251 games, led NL in strikeouts in 1968

Gibson, Josh: Negro Leagues catcher

Gibson, Kirk: All-Star outfielder, spent 17 seasons in the majors, and was the 1988 NL MVP

Giles, Brian: All-Star outfielder and lifetime .295 hitter through 2006

Giles, Warren: National League president

Gilliam, Jim: 14-year veteran and two-time All-Star, won the 1953 Rookie of the Year Award

Gilman, Richard: writer

Gilmartin, Joe: sportswriter

Glaus, Troy: four-time All-Star third baseman and MVP of the 2002 World Series

Gleason, Kid: big-league manager whose 1919 White Sox "fixed" the World Series, he also played 22 seasons in the majors

Golenbock, Peter: baseball author

Gomez, Lefty: colorful big-league pitcher

Gomez, Preston: former big-league manager who twice relieved a pitcher working on a late no-hitter

Gonzalez, Fredi: major league manager and coach

Gonzalez, Luis: nicknamed "Gonzo," 17-year outfielder who hit 596 doubles

Gordon, Joe: manager, played 11 seasons at second base and was the 1942 AL MVP

Gott, Jim: pitched 14 seasons in the majors and recorded 91 saves

Gould, Stephen Jay: writer

Gowdy, Hank: catcher for 17 seasons, hit a career-high .317 in 1922

Grabarkewitz, Billy: infielder, member of the 1970 NL All-Star team

Graham, Frank: sportswriter

Griffey, Ken Jr.: Hall of Fame outfielder who was the 1997 AL MVP, a seven-time Silver Slugger Award winner, and a 10-time Gold Glove winner

Grimes, Burleigh: Hall of Fame pitcher, led his league twice in wins and won 270 career games

Grimm, Charlie: big-league manager who won 1,287 games and was a former first baseman

Groat, Dick: MVP in 1960, five-time All-Star shortstop, standout basketball player at Duke

Groh, Heinie: played 16 seasons, mainly at third, and played in five World Series, twice led the NL in on-base percentage

Guerrero, Pedro: outfielder/infielder, .300 lifetime hitter

Guidry, Ron: All-Star pitcher, had a glittering .651 won-loss percentage

Guillen, Carlos: infielder who played 14 seasons, three-time All-Star

Gumbel, Bryant: television personality

Guthrie, Bill: major league umpire

Gwynn, Tony: Padres superstar outfielder for 20 seasons and member of the 3,000-hit club

H

Hack, Stan: former third baseman and manager, was an All-Star who appeared in four World Series

Haddix, Harvey: major league pitcher of 14 seasons, three-time All-Star

Halberstam, David: writer

Hall, Mel: major league outfielder for 13 years, hit .276 for his career

Haller, Tom: veteran catcher and three-time All-Star

Haney, Fred: major league manager, won the 1957 World Series

Hano, Arnold: author

Hargrove, Mike: All-Star first baseman and manager, nicknamed "the Human Rain Delay"

Harrelson, Bud: shortstop for 16 seasons, once won a Gold Glove award

Harrelson, Ken: major league outfielder and announcer

Harris, Bucky: Hall of Famer, won 2,157 games as a manager

Harris, Mickey: pitcher for nine seasons between 1940 and 1952, one-time All-Star

Harrison, James R.: writer

Harvey, Doug: umpire

Harwell, Ernie: Hall of Fame announcer

Hassler, Andy: 14-year journeyman pitcher

Hatton, Grady: played for 12 seasons, mainly as an infielder, managed the Astros

Hayworth, Ray: caught 15 seasons, primarily with the Tigers

Heaverlo, Dave: pitcher with a lifetime 26–26 record

Held, Woodie: 14-year veteran infielder/outfielder

Helton, Todd: 17-year first baseman, four-time winner of the Silver Slugger Award, .316 lifetime batting average

Henderson, Dave: 14 year outfielder, All-Star in 1991

Henderson, Rickey: Hall of Fame outfielder, led league in stolen bases 12 times and his lifetime total of 1,406 stolen bases is the best ever

Hendricks, Elrod: veteran catcher and major league coach

Henrich, Tommy: New York Yankees outfielder for 11 seasons, an All-Star who once drove in 100 runs

Hentgen, Pat: All-Star pitcher and 14-year veteran who won the 1996 Cy Young Award

Herman, Babe: Major League outfielder, hit .324 lifetime with 997 RBIs

Herman, Billy: Hall of Fame second baseman, led NL in hits in 1935

Herzog, Whitey: World Series–winning manager

Higgins, Pinky: third baseman who was a three-time All-Star and went on to manage for the Red Sox

Hodges, Gil: Brooklyn star first baseman, eight-time All-Star who appeared in seven World Series, managed 1969 Mets to world championship

Holmes, Tommy: former All-Star outfielder, minor league manager, once led NL in home runs

Holtzman, Ken: member of the champion Oakland A's from 1972 to 1974

Honig, Donald: sportswriter

Hoover, Herbert: former president of the US

Hornsby, Rogers: hit .358 lifetime, Hall of Fame second baseman

Horton, Willie: played 18 seasons primarily for the Tigers, outfielder/designated hitter, four-time All-Star

Hough, Charlie: pitched 25 Major League seasons, posting a 216–216 record

Householder, Paul: played from 1980 through 1987 as an outfielder, mainly for the Reds

Hovley, Steve: former big-league outfielder

Howard, Chris: older brother of slugger Ryan Howard

Howard, Elston: All-Star catcher who was the 1963 MVP and appeared in 10 World Series, mainly as a Yankee

Howsam, Bob: big-league baseball executive

Hoyt, Waite: major league pitcher, won 237 games, member of the Hall of Fame

Hrabosky, Al: Relief pitcher with 13 years in the majors, once led league in saves

Hubbell, Carl: Hall of Fame pitcher of 16 seasons with the Giants, won 253 games

Huggins, Miller: Hall of Fame manager, former player, led three Yankees teams to World Series wins

Hunt, Ron: infielder and former record holder for most times hit by a pitch

Hunter, Jim: known as "Catfish," Hall of Fame pitcher, had a lifetime ERA of 3.26

Hurdle, Clint: former outfielder and major league manager

Hutchinson, Fred: big-league manager for 12 seasons, won the pennant in 1961 with the Reds, pitched for the Tigers

I

Irvin, Monte: Hall of Fame outfielder of the Negro Leagues, spent seven seasons with the New York Giants, hit .293 lifetime

Izenberg, Jerry: sportswriter

J

Jackson, Reverend Jesse: civil rights activist

Jackson, Joe: lifetime .356 hitter banned from Hall of Fame consideration due to his involvement in the 1919 Black Sox scandal

Jackson, Reggie: outfielder/designated hitter and member of the Hall of Fame

James, Bill: baseball analyst and writer

James, Bill: pitcher who won 26 games for the 1914 Miracle Braves

Jaramillo, Rudy: highly regarded hitting coach

Jenkins, Fergie: won 284 games and the 1971 Cy Young Award, was a seven-time 20-game winner

Jennings, Hughie: big-league manager

Jeter, Derek: All-Star shortstop and veteran of seven World Series

John, Tommy: All-Star pitcher, winner of 288 games lifetime

Johnson, Ban: American League president

Johnson, Davey: former All-Star second baseman who once hit 43 homers, later became World Series–winning manager

Johnson, Harry: known as "Steamboat," former major league umpire

Johnson, Howard: All-Star third baseman and member of the 30-30 club

Johnson, Randy: Hall of Fame pitcher who won 303 games, threw a perfect game, and won five Cy Young Awards

Johnson, Walter: Hall of Fame pitcher who won 417 games with a season high of 36

Jones, Chipper: All-Star infielder/outfielder, won the 1999 NL MVP

Jones, Todd: 16-year closer with 319 saves

Jorgensen, Mike: first baseman, winner of the 1973 NL Gold Glove Award

Justice, David: outfielder for 14 seasons and 1990 Rookie of the Year

K

Kaat, Jim: winner of 16 Gold Glove Awards and 283 games, three-time All-Star

Kahn, Roger: sportswriter and author

Kaline, Al: Hall of Fame outfielder for the Detroit Tigers, member of the 3,000-hit club

Kanehl, Rod: former major league infielder

Keane, Johnny: big-league manager of six seasons, won the 1964 World Series with the Cardinals

Kearney, Bob: caught for eight seasons between 1979 and 1987

Kelly, Roberto: outfielder for 14 seasons and two-time All-Star

Kelly, Tom: major league manager, won two World Series

Kennedy, Terry: catcher and four-time All-Star

Kern, Jim: major league pitcher, worked mainly in relief for 13 years

Key, Jimmy: pitched from 1984 to 1998, winning 186 games

Killebrew, Harmon: Hall of Famer whose 573 homers stands 12th all time, 1969 MVP

Kindred, Dave: sportswriter

Kiner, Ralph: outfielder, led National League in homers seven consecutive seasons, later became a baseball announcer

King, Jim: Chicago Cubs outfielder

King, Larry: talk show host

Kirksey, George: sportswriter

Kissinger, Henry: former US secretary of state

Klem, Bill: major league umpire

Kluszewski, Ted: first baseman nicknamed "Big Klu," compiled 1,028 RBIs, a four-time All-Star

Koppett, Leonard: sportswriter

Kornheiser, Tony: writer for the *Washington Post*

Kostro, Frank: a utilityman for seven big-league seasons

Koufax, Sandy: ace southpaw, member of the Hall of Fame, posted a .655 WL%

Kranepool, Ed: member of the 1969 Miracle Mets, played 18 seasons, mainly at first base

Kruk, John: All-Star outfielder and television analyst

Kubek, Tony: Yankees shortstop and three-time All-Star; announcer

Kuhn, Bowie: former major league commissioner

L

LaMonte, Bob: baseball agent

Lamp, Dennis: major league pitcher

Lane, Frank: major league team executive

LaPoint, Dave: 12-year veteran pitcher

Lardner, Ring: sportswriter

La Russa, Tony: World Series–winning manager, former infielder

Lasorda, Tommy: Los Angeles Dodgers coach and World Series–winning manager, pitched briefly in the majors

Lau, Charlie: former catcher and legendary hitting instructor

Law, Vernon: major league pitcher

Lee, Bill: major league pitcher, famous for his zany ways, won 119 games over 14 seasons

Lefebvre, Jim: infielder and big-league manager

Leiter, Al: former pitcher of 19 years, won 162 games, and was a two-time All-Star

Lemon, Bob: major league pitching standout and manager, member of the Hall of Fame

Leonard, Dennis: pitched 12 seasons, all with the Royals, winning 144 times

Leonard, John: writer

Lewis, Joe E.: comedian

Leyland, Jim: World Series–winning manager

Lieb, Fred: sportswriter

Linn, Ed: author

Linz, Phil: New York Yankees utility player

Lis, Joe: played eight seasons, mainly at first base, from 1970 through 1977

Lockhart, Toki: grandmother of pitcher Len Barker

Lockwood, Skip: pitched a dozen seasons for five different clubs, recorded 68 saves

Loes, Billy: pitcher, appeared in three World Series for Brooklyn

Logan, Johnny: major league shortstop, a member of the 1957 champion Braves team

Lolich, Mickey: major league pitcher, won three World Series games in 1968

Lombardi, Ernie: Hall of Fame catcher who twice led his league in hitting and won the 1938 MVP

Lonborg, Jim: 15-year veteran pitcher, All-Star in 1967, the year he won two World Series games

Lopez, Al: Hall of Fame catcher/manager, caught 19 seasons, as a manager he won 1,410 games

Lowenstein, John: former outfielder/designated hitter

Luciano, Ron: major league umpire and author of several books

Lyle, Sparky: ace reliever and Cy Young Award winner, most famous for his stay with the Yankees

Lyons, Ted: Hall of Famer and winner of 260 games

M

Mack, Connie: owner and manager of the Philadelphia A's

Maddox, Garry: nicknamed the "Secretary of Defense," Gold Glove Award winner 1975 to 1982

Maglie, Sal: pitched 10 seasons, making the All-Star team in 1951 and 1952, nicknamed "the Barber," notorious for brushing back and hitting batters

Magrane, Joe: pitched eight years in the majors, led NL in ERA in 1988

Malamud, Bernard: author

Mantei, Matt: closer, had a single season high of 32 saves

Mantle, David: son of Mickey

Mantle, Mickey: Yankees great and Hall of Famer, blasted 536 homers, most ever by a switch hitter

Marion, Marty: nicknamed "the Octopus," the 13-year veteran shortstop was an eight-time All-Star

Maris, Roger: broke Babe Ruth's single season home run record with 61 in 1961

Marquard, Rube: Hall of Fame pitcher of 18 seasons, winner of 201 games, appeared in five World Series

Marshall, Bob: author

Marshall, Mike: durable relief pitcher who won the Cy Young Award in 1974

Martin, Billy: infielder and fiery major league manager, most famous for his days with Yanks

Martinez, Carmelo: played 1,003 games mainly as an outfielder, his career high was 21 homers

Martinez, Edgar: All-Star designated hitter, .312 lifetime hitter

Martinez, Teddy: infielder who spent nine seasons in the majors

Martinez, Tino: All-Star first baseman, won one Silver Slugger Award

Masterson, Walter: pitched 14 seasons, mainly for Washington, made two All-Star teams

Mathews, Eddie: third baseman who slugged 512 homers over 17 seasons, member of the Hall of Fame

Mathewson, Christy: Hall of Fame pitcher nicknamed "Big Six," winner of 373 games

Mauch, Gene: won 1,902 games as a manager

May, Lee: 18-year veteran first baseman, led AL in RBIs in 1976

Mayberry, John: first baseman, played 15 seasons, hit a personal high of 34 HR in 1975

Mays, Willie: Hall of Fame outfielder who drilled 660 homers and drove home 1,903 runs

Mazeroski, Bill: All-Star second baseman and Hall of Famer, hit Series-winning home run in 1960

McCarthy, Joe: Hall of Fame manager, won nine pennants and 2,125 games

McCarver, Tim: major league catcher and announcer, appeared in the 1964, '67 and '68 World Series

McCatty, Steve: pitched for Oakland for nine seasons, lifetime record 63–63

McConnell, Dorothy C.: writer

McCovey, Willie: Hall of Fame first baseman who hit 521 homers over 22 seasons

McCraw, Tom: coach and former infielder/outfielder

McDowell, Sam: also known as "Sudden Sam," five-time strikeout king

McGlothen, Lynn: pitcher for 11 seasons, All-Star in 1974 when he won a personal high of 16 games

McGraw, John: Hall of Famer, won 2,763 games as a manager including three World Series

McGraw, Tug: major league pitcher, 180 saves in 19 years, appeared in two World Series

McKeon, Jack: managed five big-league clubs, taking the Florida Marlins to the 2003 world championship

McLemore, Mark: veteran of 19 seasons, collected 1,602 hits

McMahon, Don: All-Star pitcher, spent 18 years in the majors, later a pitching coach

McNally, Dave: All-Star pitcher, spent 14 seasons in the majors, won a personal high of 24 games in 1970

McRae, Hal: designated hitter/outfielder, won a 1982 Silver Slugger Award

Meany, Tom: sportswriter

Medwick, Joe: lifetime .324 hitter, member of the Hall of Fame, won the Triple Crown in 1937, his MVP season

Messersmith, Andy: pitcher for 12 seasons, appeared in the 1974 World Series and led the NL in wins in 1974

Meyer, Billy: managed the Pittsburgh Pirates for five seasons

Michaels, Al: broadcaster

Miller, Ray: pitching coach and manager of the Twins and Orioles

Minaya, Omar: baseball general manager, most notably for the Mets

Minoso, Minnie: All-Star outfielder of 17 seasons and three-time Gold Glove winner

Miranda, Willie: played infield, mainly shortstop, for nine seasons

Mize, Johnny: Hall of Fame first baseman, led NL in slugging and home runs four times

Mizell, Vinegar Bend: pitched for nine seasons, winner of 90 games, pitched in the 1960 World Series for the Pirates

Monday, Rick: major league outfielder, two-time All-Star, also famous for rescuing an American flag protestors were about to burn

Morgan, Joe: Hall of Fame second baseman of 22 seasons, hit 268 career homers, won five Gold Gloves, and was a two-time MVP

Morris, Jack: All-Star pitcher who won 254 games and was the World Series MVP in 1991

Muncrief, Bob: pitched 12 seasons in the major leagues winning 80 contests

Murcer, Bobby: All-Star outfielder, hit 252 homers over his 17 seasons in the majors

Murray, Jim: sportswriter and winner of the 1987 Spink Award

Murtaugh, Danny: former infielder and manager, won two World Series as a manager

Musial, Stan: nicknamed "the Man," compiled 3,630 hits over 22 seasons, member of the Hall of Fame

N

Nagy, Charles: pitcher, mainly for Cleveland, three-time All-Star

Narron, Sam: major league catcher for three seasons, but played in only 24 games

Nettles, Graig: All-Star third baseman, Gold Glove winner

Newhouser, Hal: Hall of Fame pitcher of 17 seasons, mainly with Detroit

Niedenfuer, Tom: veteran pitcher of 10 seasons, member of the 1981 World Series–winning Dodgers

Niekro, Phil: Hall of Fame pitcher who won 318 games and received the 1980 Roberto Clemente Award

Nipper, Al: pitcher for seven seasons, his record was 46–50 lifetime

Novikoff, Lou: outfielder, played five seasons, mainly for the Cubs, between 1941 and 1946

O

O'Donnell, Bob: author

O'Farrell, Bob: former catcher who hit .324 in 1922, later became a manager

O'Malley, Walter: former owner of the Dodgers

O'Neil, Buck: popular star of the Negro Leagues, first baseman

O'Neill, Steve: former big-league catcher and manager

Ortiz, Junior: catcher for 13 seasons, .256 lifetime hitter

Osteen, Claude: won 196 games and had a 3.30 career ERA, was a three-time All-Star

Ott, Ed: caught eight seasons, seven for the Pirates

Owens, Paul: managed three years with the Phillies

Ozark, Danny: big-league manager who won 618 games

P

Paciorek, Tom: hit .282 lifetime, first baseman/outfielder and announcer

Pafko, Andy: All-Star outfielder, played 17 seasons, hit .285 lifetime

Paige, Satchel: star pitcher of the Negro Leagues and Major League Baseball as the oldest rookie ever

Pagliaroni, Jim: caught for 11 seasons and was a .252 lifetime hitter

Palmer, Jim: Hall of Fame pitcher, winner of 268 games over 19 seasons, all with the O's

Parker, Dave: former two-time batting champ, 1978 MVP, strong-armed outfielder

Passarella, Art: major league umpire

Patterson, Bob: pitched 13 seasons, appeared in the NLCS in 1990, '91, and '92

Paul, Gabe: major league executive

Pepitone, Joe: first baseman/outfielder, three-time Gold Glove winner who appeared in two World Series for the Yankees

Perry, Gaylord: 300-game winner and member of the Hall of Fame

Perry, Gerald: outfielder and major league coach, All-Star in 1988

Pesky, Johnny: manager, infielder, led AL in singles three times

Pettis, Gary: five-time Gold Glove–winning outfielder, veteran of 11 seasons

Phillips, B. J.: writer

Phillips, Lefty: managed the Angels for three seasons

Phillips, Tony: versatile veteran of 18 seasons, twice led the AL in walks drawn

Piazza, Mike: Hall of Fame catcher who has collected 2,127 hits, owns a .308 lifetime batting average, and was a 12-time All-Star

Piersall, Jimmy: big-league outfielder, an All-Star, and a Gold Glove winner

Piniella, Lou: major league outfielder, manager, part-time television analyst

Pipp, Wally: major league first baseman who lost his job to Lou Gehrig

Plimpton, George: author

Pole, Dick: coach and former pitcher, mainly for the Red Sox, won 25 games lifetime

Porter, Ross: announcer

Povich, Shirley: sportswriter

Power, Vic: mainly a first baseman for 12 seasons, hit .284 lifetime and was a four-time All-Star

Prince, Bob: Pittsburgh Pirates broadcaster

Pratt, Todd: caught 553 games in the majors

Puckett, Kirby: Hall of Fame outfielder, hit .318 lifetime

Puhl, Terry: outfielder for 15 seasons and All-Star in 1978

Q

Quigley, Martin: writer

Quisenberry, Dan: Kansas City closer

R

Radatz, Dick: pitched seven seasons and was a two-time All-Star

Radcliffe, Theodore "Double Duty": caught and pitched in the Negro Leagues

Rader, Doug: third baseman who won five Gold Gloves and went on to manage three big league clubs

Randle, Lenny: 12-year veteran infielder/outfielder, twice stole 30 or more bases

Randolph, Willie: former All-Star second baseman, played 18 seasons, coached and managed

Raschi, Vic: pitched 10 seasons, had a WL% of .667, and was in six World Series

Reardon, Beans: major league umpire

Reed, Steve: relief pitcher of 14 seasons, led NL in games in 1994

Reese, Pee Wee: shortstop for 2,014 games, 10-time All-Star, member of the Hall of Fame

Reinsdorf, Jerry: major league team executive

Reiser, Pete: Former Dodgers player and coach, hit .295 lifetime, mainly as an outfielder

Rettenmund, Merv: former outfielder and big-league coach, hit .271 over 13 seasons

Reuss, Jerry: won 220 games over a 22-year stint in the majors

Reynolds, Allie: nicknamed "the Superchief," he won 182 games with a .630 WL%

Rice, Grantland: sportswriter

Richards, Paul: baseball scout, manager, and executive

Rickey, Branch: baseball executive

Rigney, Bill: veteran manager and winner of 1,239 games

Ripken, Billy: mainly a second baseman, played 12 big-league seasons, brother of Cal Ripken Jr.

Ripken, Cal Jr.: owns record for most consecutive games played, compiled 3,184 hits over 21 seasons

Ritter, Lawrence S.: sportswriter

Rivers, Mickey: veteran of 15 seasons, All-Star outfielder who hit a career-high .333 in 1980

Rizzuto, Phil: Yankee Hall of Famer and announcer

Roberts, Robin: Hall of Fame pitcher, winner of 286 games, and two-time *The Sporting News* Pitcher of the Year

Robinson, Arthur: New York writer

Robinson, Brooks: All-Star Orioles third baseman who won 16 Gold Gloves, Hall of Famer

Robinson, Frank: Hall of Fame outfielder, member of the 500 home run club

Robinson, Jackie: broke baseball's color barrier, Dodgers standout, Hall of Famer since 1962

Rodriguez, Alex: shortstop/third baseman, three-time MVP, 696 lifetime HR

Roe, Preacher: big-league pitcher, .602 WL% for his 12-year career, mainly with Brooklyn

Rogers, Kenny: won 219 games through 2006 and five Gold Gloves

Rogers, Will: humorist

Rogovin, Saul: pitcher with a lifetime record of 48–48

Rolen, Scott: All-Star third baseman played 17 seasons and was an All-Star seven times, won eight Gold Gloves

Roosevelt, Franklin Delano: former president of the US

Rose, Pete: all-time hit leader with 4,256, played 24 seasons, scored 2,165 runs

Rose, Pete Jr.: son of Pete Rose who played 11 big-league games

Rosen, Al: 1953 MVP, led AL in homers and RBIs twice

Rowe, Schoolboy: pitcher for 15 seasons, had a .610 WL%, appeared in three World Series for the Tigers

Ruffing, Red: Hall of Fame pitcher who won 273 games and once led his league in wins

Ruth, Babe: legendary slugger who hit 714 home runs and was a charter member of the Hall of Fame

Ryan, Connie: infielder, coach, and manager

S

Saberhagen, Bret: 16-year veteran pitcher and two-time Cy Young Award winner

Sadecki, Ray: veteran pitcher, appeared in two World Series

Sage, George H.: writer

Salisbury, Luke: author

Santo, Ron: Hall of Famer played 15 seasons, 14 with the Cubs, hit 342 home runs and was a nine-time All-Star

Saroyan, William: playwright and author

Sawyer, Eddie: big-league manager with 817 games experience

Sax, Steve: Five-time All-Star second baseman, hit .281 lifetime, appeared in two World Series

Sayles, John: author

Scheffing, Bob: former big-league manager of six seasons with the Cubs and Tigers

Schilling, Curt: All-Star pitcher, won 216 games in 20 seasons, twice led league in wins

Schmidt, Mike: Hall of Fame third baseman, 18-year veteran who hit 548 home runs

Schoendienst, Red: former World Series–winning manager and second baseman, member of the Hall of Fame, played in three World Series

Schuerholz, John: baseball general manager, most successfully with the Braves

Schultz, Joe: Seattle Pilots manager in their only season

Schultz, Barney: won 20 games over seven seasons and appeared in the 1964 World Series

Scioscia, Mike: All-Star catcher who played from 1980 to 1992, appeared in two World Series, manager who won the 2002 World Series

Scott, George: first baseman who hit 271 home runs lifetime and was a three-time All-Star

Scully, Vin: Dodgers announcer

Seaver, Tom: Hall of Fame pitcher, won three Cy Young Awards and led league in ERA three times, had 311 victories over 20 seasons

Seymour, Harold: author, PhD, and former big-league scout

Shamsky, Art: played eight seasons, mainly in the outfield, hit a career-high 21 homers in 1966

Shannon, Mike: former big leaguer of nine seasons, was a member of the pennant-winning Cardinals of '64, '67 and '68

Sharon, Dick: outfielder, played three seasons

Shaughnessy, Dan: Boston sportswriter

Sheffield, Gary: outfielder/infielder slugged 509 homers

Sherry, Larry: pitcher with 11 years experience, appeared in the 1959 World Series where he registered an 0.71 ERA

Showalter, Buck: big-league manager, winner of 1,551 games

Shriver, Chuck: former team publicist for the Cubs

Shuba, George: spent seven seasons between 1948 and 1955 with the Brooklyn Dodgers as an outfielder

Shuey, Paul: spent 10 years in the majors as a relief pitcher

Simmons, Lon: Oakland A's announcer

Simmons, Ted: Hall of Fame catcher, .285 lifetime hitter with 248 HR, drove in 100 three times

Sims, Duke: caught for 11 seasons

Skinner, Bob: two-time All-Star, hit .321 in 1958 for the Pirates

Slaughter, Enos: outfielder, nicknamed "Country," voted into Hall of Fame in 1985

Smalley, Roy III: All-Star shortstop, played 13 seasons and had 1,454 hits

Smalley, Roy Jr.: shortstop who played 11 seasons from 1948 to 1958

Smith, Curt: author

Smith, Dave: major league relief pitcher, racked up 216 saves over 13 seasons

Smith, Mayo: big league manager, won the 1968 World Series

Smith, Red: sportswriter, winner of the 1976 Spink Award

Smith, Reggie: switch-hitting outfielder of 17 seasons, led NL in on-base percentage in 1977

Smith, Ron: writer

Smith, Zane: pitcher of 13 seasons, winner of 100 games, once led the league in games started

Smithson, Mike: pitched eight seasons and won 76 games

Smoltz, John: eight-time All-Star, 1996 Cy Young Award winner, led NL in strikeouts twice

Spahn, Warren: Hall of Famer who won more games, 363, than any lefty ever

Spalding, Albert: baseball pioneer and member of the Hall of Fame

Speaker, Tris: Hall of Fame center fielder, 1912 MVP, all-time leader in doubles with 792

Speier, Justin: 12-year veteran pitcher

Splittorff, Paul: pitched 15 seasons for the Royals winning 166 games, pitched in the 1980 World Series

Springstead, Marty: former big-league umpire

Stanky, Eddie: All-Star infielder, manager, led league in walks drawn three times

Stanley, Mike: major league catcher, hit .270 lifetime

Stargell, Willie: outfielder/first baseman, hit 475 home runs, member of Hall of Fame

Steinbach, Terry: All-Star catcher, spent 14 seasons in the majors and appeared in three World Series

Steinbrenner, George: New York Yankees owner

Stengel, Casey: legendary player and manager, most famous for his time with the Yankees and Mets and for his colorful use (and misuse) of the language

Stewart, Dave: pitcher who won 168 games over 16 seasons and appeared in five World Series, was the MVP of the 1989 Series

Stone, Steve: All-Star pitcher, winner of the 1980 Cy Young Award

Stuart, Dick: played first base (poorly) for 10 seasons, nicknamed "Dr. Strangeglove"

Sturdivant, Tom: pitched 10 seasons, single-season high was 16 victories

Sullivan, Frank: pitched 11 seasons and was a two-time All-Star who once led his league in wins

Sutcliffe, Rick: All-Star pitcher who won the Rookie of the Year Award in 1979 and the Cy Young Award in 1984

Sutter, Bruce: Hall of Fame pitcher, saved 300 games lifetime with a high of 45, six-time All-Star and winner of a Cy Young Award

Sutton, Don: Hall of Fame pitcher, winner of 324 games

Swift, Bob: veteran catcher of 14 seasons, was behind the plate when 3'7" Eddie Gaedel came to bat

Swift, E. M.: sportswriter

Swisher, Nick: 12-year outfielder, hit a career-high 35 homers in 2006

Swoboda, Ron: outfielder for nine seasons, mostly with the Mets, hit .242 lifetime

T

Tanana, Frank: won 240 games over 21 seasons, once led the AL in strikeouts

Tanner, Chuck: big league manager who won 1,352 games, won the 1979 World Series and was a former outfielder

Tebbetts, Birdie: former catcher of 14 seasons and big league manager who won 748 games

Templeton, Garry: All-Star shortstop who led the NL in triples three times

Terry, Bill: last National Leaguer to hit .400, Hall of Famer

Terry, Ralph: pitched 12 seasons mainly with the Yankees and selected for the 1962 All-Star team

Thomas, Frank: Hall of Fame slugger known as "the Big Hurt," swatted 521 HR and drove in 1,704 runs

Thome, Jim: All-Star first baseman who hit 612 home runs and had nine 100-RBI seasons

Thompson, Fresco: baseball executive

Throneberry, Marv: noted for his poor defensive play, this first baseman lasted seven seasons in the majors

Thurber, James: author

Tiant, Luis: winner of 229 games, twice led AL in ERA

Torborg, Jeff: former catcher, manager and announcer

Torre, Joe: former MVP player, announcer, and World Series–winning manager

Trebelhorn, Tom: big-league manager mainly for the Brewers

Triandos, Gus: caught nearly 1,000 games over 13 seasons and made three All-Star teams

Trillo, Manny: All-Star second baseman, played 17 seasons, and was on four All-Star teams

Trimble, Joe: sportswriter

Trout, Dizzy: All-Star pitcher of 15 seasons mainly with the Tigers, won 170 games

Turner, Ted: Atlanta Braves team owner

Twain, Mark: American novelist

U

Ueberroth, Peter: former baseball commissioner

Uecker, Bob: Major League catcher and announcer

Underwood, Matt: baseball announcer

Updike, John: author

V

Vaccaro, Mike: columnist for the *New York Post*

Valentine, Bobby: manager and former infielder/outfielder

Valenzuela, Fernando: All-Star pitcher, veteran of 17 seasons, won both the Cy Young Award and the Rookie of the Year Award in 1981

Vander Meer, Johnny: pitched 13 years, mainly for the Reds, threw back-to-back no-hitters

Van Slyke, Andy: major league outfielder and coach

Vaughan, Bill: columnist

Vaughn, Mo: primarily a first baseman for 12 seasons, led the AL in RBIs in 1995, his MVP Award winning year

Veale, Bob: flame throwing pitcher of 13 seasons, won 120 games, and was on the 1971 world champion Pirates

Veeck, Bill: owner of several minor and major league clubs

Virdon, Bill: 12-year veteran, mainly with the Pirates, hit a career-high .319 in 1956, won one Gold Glove and later managed

W

Waddell, Rube: Hall of Fame pitcher, twice led his league in ERA and six times in strikeouts

Wagner, Billy: fireballing reliever with 422 saves in 16 seasons

Wagner, Honus: major league shortstop and Hall of Famer, drilled 3,415 hits

Wagner, Leon: outfielder for 12 seasons, made the 1962 and 1963 All-Star squads, and hit 211 lifetime homers

Walker, Harry: two-time All-Star and former big league manager

Walker, Larry: Hall of Fame outfielder, winner of seven Gold Gloves, hit .313 lifetime

Waner, Paul: Pittsburgh Pirates outfielder and Hall of Famer, banged out 3,152 hits

Washington, Claudell: All-Star outfielder, played 17 seasons, member of the 1974 world champion A's

Wathan, John: former big league catcher/first baseman for 10 seasons, managed for six years

Watson, Bob: All-Star first baseman/outfielder who hit a career-high .324 in 1975

Weaver, Earl: legendary Orioles World Series-winning manager

Weiss, Walt: smooth-fielding shortstop of 14 seasons, 1998 Rookie of the Year

Welborn, Todd: minor league pitcher

Wells, David: pitched 21 seasons, had a WL% of .604, and was a three-time All-Star

Westrum, Wes: former major league catcher and manager

White, Bill: All-Star first baseman, served as NL president, broadcaster

White, Devon: seven-time Gold Glove winner in the outfield, stole 346 bases lifetime

White, Roy: All-Star outfielder, played 15 seasons with the Yankees, and collected 1,803 hits

Whitman, Walt: poet

Wilcox, Frederick B.: writer

Wilcox, Milt: pitcher for 16 seasons and winner of 119 games

Will, George F.: writer

Williams, Bernie: All-Star outfielder, played 16 seasons hitting .297

Williams, Dick: former outfielder/infielder and manager who won two World Series with the A's

Williams, Mitch: relief pitcher, member of the 1989 NL All-Star team

Williams, Ted: Boston Red Sox superstar and Hall of Famer, hit .344 lifetime, 521 HR

Wills, Maury: All-Star shortstop, former record holder for stolen bases in a season (104) in 1962

Wilson, Glenn: outfielder and one-time All-Star, played 10 seasons, hit 98 home runs

Wilson, Hack: outfielder who drove in 191 runs in 1930, the single season record

Wilson, Willie: speedy outfielder, two-time All-Star, won a Gold Glove

Wohlford, Jim: major league outfielder, hit .260 over 15 years

Wolfe, Tom: author

Wood, Joe: pitched 11 seasons, had an ERA of 2.03, reportedly was faster than Walter Johnson

Woodling, Gene: appeared in five consecutive World Series from 1949 to 1953 and once led his league in on-base percentage

Wright, Craig R.: sportswriter

Wright, David: All-Star third baseman of the New York Mets who drove in a personal high 124 runs in 2008

Wrigley, Phil: Chicago Cubs owner

Wrona, Rick: was a catcher for six seasons and a lifetime .244 hitter

Wulf, Steve: writer

Wyatt, Whit: All-Star pitcher, spent 16 seasons in the majors and once led his league in wins

Wynn, Early: Hall of Fame pitcher, winner of 300 games, known for his intimidating ways

Y

Yastrzemski, Carl: Hall of Fame outfielder with 452 homers and 1,844 RBI

Young, Cy: Hall of Fame pitcher who won a record 511 games, fanned 2,803 men in 22 years

Z

Zachry, Pat: pitcher of 10 seasons, All-Star in 1978

Zimmer, Don: big-league player and manager

Zisk, Richie: outfielder/designated hitter, two-time All-Star

SOURCES

BOOKS

A Day in the Bleachers by Arnold Hano

And the Crowd Goes Wild by Joe Garner

And the Fans Roared by Joe Garner

The Babe and I by Mrs. Babe Ruth and Bill Slocum

The Babe: A Life in Pictures by Lawrence S. Ritter

Babe Ruth: A Biography by Wayne Stewart

Babe Ruth as I Knew Him by Waite Hoyt

The Babe Book by Ernestine Miller

Babe Ruth's Own Book of Baseball by Babe Ruth

The Babe Signed My Shoe by Ernie Harwell

Babe: The Legend Comes to Life by Robert W. Creamer

Ball Four by Jim Bouton

Baseball by George Vecsey

The Baseball Almanac by Dan Schlossberg

Baseball and the Meaning of Life Edited by Josh Leventhal

Baseball for the Love of It by Anthony J. Connor

Baseball is a Funny Game by Joe Garagiola

Baseball Oddities by Wayne Stewart

The Baseball Reader by Charles Einstein

The Best of Red Smith by Red Smith
The Big Bam by Leigh Montville
The Bill James Guide to Baseball Managers by Bill James
The Bill James Historical Baseball Abstract by Bill James
The Boys of Summer by Roger Kahn
The Bronx Zoo by Sparky Lyle and Peter Golenbock
The Bucs! The Story of the Pittsburgh Pirates by John McCollister
Bums by Peter Golenbock
Catcher in the Wry by Bob Uecker
Cobb: A Biography by Al Stump
The Complete Armchair Book of Baseball edited by John Thorn
Cooperstown Corner by Lee Allen
Diamonds by Michael Gershman
Eight Men Out by Eliot Asinof
Emperors and Idiots by Mike Vaccaro
The Era by Roger Kahn
Fathers, Sons and Baseball by Wayne Stewart
Five Seasons by Roger Angell
Game Day by Thomas Boswell
The Glory of Their Times by Lawrence S. Ritter
Eight Men Out by Eliot Asinof
The Greatest Baseball Stories Ever Told edited by Jeff Silverman
The Head Game by Roger Kahn
The History of the Baltimore Orioles by John Nichols

SOURCES

The History of the Boston Red Sox by Aaron Frisch
The History of the Boston Red Sox by Richard Rambeck
The History of the Chicago Cubs by Aaron Frisch
The History of the Chicago Cubs by Michael E. Goodman
The History of the Cleveland Indians by Richard Rambeck
The History of the Chicago Cubs by Michael E. Goodman
The History of the Houston Astros by Michael E. Goodman
The History of the Kansas City Royals by Richard Rambeck
The History of the Minnesota Twins by Aaron Frisch
The History of the Minnesota Twins by Richard Rambeck
The History of the New York Mets by Michael E. Goodman
The History of the New York Yankees by Richard Rambeck
The History of the New York Yankees by Michael E. Goodman
The History of the San Diego Padres by Michael E. Goodman
The History of the San Francisco Giants by Aaron Frisch
The History of the Seattle Mariners by Michael E. Goodman
The History of the Texas Rangers by Aaron Frisch
The History of the Toronto Blue Jays by Richard Rambeck
Hitting Secrets of the Pros by Wayne Stewart
How Life Imitates the World Series by Thomas Boswell
How the Weather Was by Roger Kahn
I Had a Hammer by Hank Aaron with Lonnie Wheeler
The Hustler's Handbook by Bill Veeck with Ed Linn
The Image of Their Greatness by Lawrence Ritter and Donald Honig

I'm Glad You Didn't Take It Personally by Jim Bouton

Indians on the Game by Wayne Stewart

In the Shadow of the Babe by Brent Kelley

The Jocks by Leonard Shecter

Late Innings by Roger Angell

Luckiest Man by Jonathan Eig

Major League Dad by Julia Ruth Stevens and Bill Gilbert

Me and the Spitter by Gaylord Perry with Bob Sudyk

Memories and Dreams /Induction 2006, a Hall of Fame publication

Memories of a Ballplayer by Bill Werber and C. Paul Rogers III

Men at Work by George F. Will

More Tales from the Dugout by Mike Shannon

My Dad, the Babe by Dorothy Ruth Pirone and Chris Martens

The National League Story by Lee Allen

The New Thinking Man's Guide to Baseball by Leonard Koppett

Nice Guys Finish Last by Leo Durocher and Ed Linn

No Cheering in the Press Box recorded and edited by Jerome Holtzman

Baseball Oddities by Wayne Stewart

Once More Around the Park by Roger Angell

Out-of-Left-Field Baseball Trivia by Robert Obojski and Wayne Stewart

Out of My League by George Plimpton

The Pitcher by John Thorn and John Holway

Pitching Secrets of the Pros by Wayne Stewart

Rain Delays by Burt Sugar

Red Smith on Baseball compiled by Phyllis W. Smith

The Red Smith Reader edited by Dave Anderson

Ringside Seat at the Circus by Larry Merchant

The Seventh Game by Barry Levenson

The Suitors of Spring by Pat Jordan

The Summer Game by Roger Angell

Summer of '49 by David Halberstam

Tales from the Ballpark by Mike Shannon

A Thinking Man's Guide to Baseball by Leonard Koppett

This Side of Cooperstown by Larry Moffi

The Umpire Strikes Back by Ron Luciano

Veeck as in Wreck by Bill Veeck with Ed Linn

Webster's New World Dictionary of Quotable Definitions

Willie Mays: My Life in and Out of Baseball by Charles Einstein

Winning! by Earl Weaver

Young Babe Ruth by Brother Gilbert

WEBSITES

www.baseballalmanac.com

www.baseballhalloffame.org

www.mlb.com

www.webcircle.com

NEWSPAPERS

Arizona Republic

Associated Press

Baltimore Sun

Boston Globe

Chronicle-Telegram

Detroit Free Press

Newsday

New York Daily News

New York Times

Plain Dealer

USA Today

Washington Post

MAGAZINES

Baseball Digest

Inside Sports

Newsweek

Sport

Sporting News

Sports Illustrated

Time

USA Today Sports Weekly

ACKNOWLEDGMENTS

To the wonderful staff of the Lorain Public Library for all their help not only on this project, but on all of my books. A special thanks to my editor, Mark Weinstein, and to my wife, Nancy, for their assistance as well.